Saddam's War

An Iraqi Military Perspective of the Iran-Iraq War

Kevin M. Woods, Williamson Murray, and Thomas Holaday

with Mounir Elkhamri

McNair Paper 70

D1526463

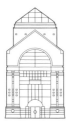

INSTITUTE FOR NATIONAL STRATEGIC STUDIES

NATIONAL DEFENSE UNIVERSITY

WASHINGTON, D.C.

2009

The opinions, conclusions, and recommendations expressed or implied within are those of the authors and do not necessarily represent the views of the Department of Defense or any other agency of the Federal Government. This publication is cleared for public release; distribution unlimited.

Except for the maps on pages 47, 51, 52, and 68, portions of this work may be quoted or reprinted without permission, provided that a standard source credit line is included. NDU Press would appreciate a courtesy copy of reprints or reviews.

This work was conducted under contract DASW01-04-C-003, Task ET-8-2579 for the National Intelligence Council. The publication of this IDA document does not indicate endorsement by the Department of Defense, nor should the contents be construed as reflecting the official position of the Agency.

© 2007, 2008 Institute for Defense Analyses, 4850 Mark Center Drive, Alexandria, Virginia 22311-1882 • (703) 845-2000.

This material may be reproduced by or for the U.S. Government pursuant to the copyright license under the clause at DFARS 252.227-7013 (Nov 95).

First printing, March 2009

ISSN 1071–7552

NDU Press publications are sold by the U.S. Government Printing Office. For ordering information, call (202) 512-1800 or write to the Superintendent of Documents, U.S. Government Printing Office, Washington, DC 20402. For the U.S. Government On-line Bookstore, go to:

<http://www.access.gpo.gov/su_docs/sale.html>.

For current publications of the Institute for National Strategic Studies, go to the NDU Press Web site at: <ndupress.ndu.edu>.

Contents

Part Two

The Interviews.

Iraqi Counterinfiltration • Iranian Militias • Iraqi Military Developments since 1991 • Cooptation of Tribes

Figures

Foreword

When lessons learned from the major combat operations phase of Operation *Iraqi Freedom* were briefed to the Nation's top leaders, the question was asked: "How did events leading to the fall of Saddam Hussein's regime look from the Iraqi perspective?" That question was posed to the Joint Advanced Warfighting Program at the Institute for Defense Analyses, triggering the Iraqi Perspectives Project (IPP), a research effort sponsored by the U.S. Joint Forces Command that has delivered several volumes of analysis and supporting materials, with more in production.

The IPP is reminiscent of an effort begun in 1946, when a team of U.S. Army historians and intelligence officers established a relationship with former members of the German General Staff to develop an understanding of familiar events from an unfamiliar point of view. This volume marks the extension of that same methodology under a different sponsor, the National Intelligence Council, to encompass a broader spectrum of Middle Eastern military history from the perspective of Lieutenant General Ra'ad Hamdani, who during Operation *Iraqi Freedom* commanded Saddam Hussein's II Republican Guard Corps. Interviewed over a number of days by project leader Kevin Woods and historian Williamson "Wick" Murray, General Hamdani shared his knowledge about a wide range of subjects, with particular emphasis on his experiences in Iraq's long war against Iran.

The project's objective was to produce a series of personal, organizational, and campaign histories of contemporary Iraq. This volume is the first in that series, provided with the hope that it will improve our understanding of Middle Eastern military thought, the new Iraqi military, neighboring countries, and the dynamics of a region of the world that is vital to U.S. interests.

Karl Lowe, Director
Joint Advanced Warfighting Division
Institute for Defense Analyses

Preface

This paper was prepared under the task order Study on Military History (Project 1946) for the National Intelligence Council. It helps address the task order objectives of:

■ developing a series of personal, organizational, and campaign histories of contemporary Iraq

■ improving and expanding our understanding of Iraq and its region

■ providing national security organizations with historical background material, political and personality profiles of the region, and data for long-term studies and analysis

■ illuminating the effects and utility of U.S. capabilities as seen by an adversary for doctrine and force developers

■ supporting strategic and operational planning by improving U.S. understanding of Arab military thought, the new Iraqi military, neighboring countries, and regional dynamics.

The Joint Advanced Warfighting Program (JAWP) was established at the Institute for Defense Analyses (IDA) and as part of the Joint Advanced Warfighting Division to serve as a catalyst for stimulating innovation and breakthrough change. It is cosponsored by the Under Secretary of Defense for Acquisition, Technology, and Logistics; the Under Secretary of Defense for Policy; the Vice Chairman of the Joint Chiefs of Staff; and the Commander, U.S. Joint Forces Command (USJFCOM). JAWP includes military personnel on joint assignments from each Service and civilian specialists from IDA. The program is located in Alexandria, Virginia, and includes an office in Norfolk, Virginia, to facilitate coordination with USJFCOM.

This paper does not necessarily reflect the views of IDA or the sponsors of JAWP. Our intent is to stimulate ideas, discussion, and, ultimately, the discovery and innovation that must fuel successful transformation.

Introduction

I n 1946, a team of U.S. Army historians and intelligence officers established a long-term exchange with a select group of former members of the German General Staff. This program supported the development of personal, organizational, and campaign histories of the German military, dramatically increasing the U.S. military's understanding of World War II.

In addition to providing an invaluable look at American military capabilities through the eyes of its most recent adversary, these former German officers constituted a special kind of red team to help the Army think through the challenges of force and doctrine development on a potential "new Eastern Front." Who better to describe what it was like to fight the Soviet Army, outnumbered, defensively, in Europe than the recently defeated Germans? The program's diverse and long-lasting impacts are evident in such projects as the acclaimed official *U.S. Army in World War II* history series (the "Green Books"), development of early Cold War military doctrines, and the campaign monographs that informed U.S. operations into the late 1990s in the Balkans.

Figure 1. **Franz Halder, former Chief of the General Staff of the German Army in World War II**

Project 1946

Sixty years later, the U.S. Government has another rare chance to examine doctrine, intelligence, operations, and strategy through the lens of a recent military opponent. The Iraqi Perspectives Project (IPP) demonstrated the potential of combining interviews of former Iraqi senior leaders with captured Iraqi documents, augmented by detailed knowledge of American operations on the ground and in the air.[1] This "quick look" history and its accompanying operational analysis represent an attempt to understand a substantial part of contemporary history in the Middle East. By leveraging the concept first used with German officers following World War II, the IPP has expanded to encompass an additional sponsor, to address more topics, and to answer a wider range of operational questions.

Named "Project 1946," this expanded effort can help develop a deeper understanding of the region's future by examining its recent past. An exchange with former senior Iraqi military leaders opens up a wealth of knowledge of operational experience in the 1973 Arab-Israeli War, campaigns against the Kurds, the Iran-Iraq War,

Figure 2. **General Ra'ad Hamdani (left), former Iraqi Republican Guard Corps commander, explains details of the 1986 Iranian capture of Al-Fao to members of the Project 1946 research team**

Operation *Desert Storm,* the 1991 uprisings, military operations and adaptations under sanctions, and Operation *Iraqi Freedom.* Moreover, such new knowledge can provide valuable insights into the political, strategic, military, and cultural dynamics of the Middle East.

The task for Project 1946 is to develop a series of personal, organizational, and campaign histories of contemporary Iraq's military. Broadly speaking, these histories, when augmented by archival and open source research, will greatly expand the understanding of Iraq and the surrounding region. Moreover, such professional exchanges can fill gaps in the historical record, develop a richer set of political and personality profiles in the region, and provide data for other long-term studies and analyses. In a narrower vein, Project 1946 can illuminate, for doctrine and force developers, the effects and utility of certain U.S. capabilities as seen by an adversary. Finally, material derived from this study can support strategic and operational planning by improving the general understanding of Arab military thought, military capabilities, selected countries, and regional dynamics. Future Project 1946 deliverables are expected to include a series of monographs and oral histories taken from interviews of former Iraqi military personnel, periodic summaries of Iraqi monographs and oral histories, and a database for additional research.

Organization of This Paper

This McNair Paper is divided into two parts. Part One is a summary of the major insights as interpreted by the authors based on their interviews of General Hamdani. Part Two presents the detailed, edited transcriptions of the 16 interview sessions. The interviews are presented in the order in which they occurred and generally follow the historical course of events. To help the reader, the major themes of each discussion are listed at the beginning of each interview session and are indexed alphabetically after the last discussion. A short bibliography is also included.

Part One.
Summary and Analysis

The purpose of Project 1946 is to develop a deeper and broader understanding of Middle Eastern military art and science. This project, like the similar post–World War II projects that inspired it, aims at exploring recent military history and culture by examining the documentary record and interviewing participants from the "other side of the hill." This perspective may or may not reflect events as they were or potentially will be. Nevertheless, just as the deliberate study of the German military experience 60 years ago positively affected early Cold War capabilities, Project 1946 (and similar efforts) can potentially improve ongoing and future analyses of the Middle East in the wake of Operation *Iraqi Freedom*.[2]

A small team of researchers from the Institute for Defense Analyses (IDA) and the U.S. Army's Foreign Military Studies Office traveled to Jordan and conducted 16 hours of formal interviews and 8 hours of informal discussions with Lieutenant General Ra'ad Hamdani (formerly a corps commander in Saddam Hussein's Republican Guard). General Hamdani's long career as a professional soldier spanned Iraq's participation in the 1973 Arab-Israeli War and ended with his command of the II Republican Guard Corps during the defense of Baghdad in Operation *Iraqi Freedom*.[3] The specific topical focus of this research effort was Iraq's war with Iran (1980–1988) and the potential for war with Iran after 1988.

General Comments

The discussions with General Hamdani provided insights ranging from the nature of Saddam's regime and its civil-military relations to the conduct of the Iran-Iraq War, and finally to the weaknesses within the Iranian approach to war both in the 1980s and beyond. Throughout the discussions, he displayed the strengths and weaknesses of his background, particularly the strengths. Hamdani is a Baghdad-born Sunni Arab who is comfortable with and committed to a secular state. In most respects, he is a consummate professional with a solid grasp of the day-to-day details of competent military leadership, as well as a considerable mastery of the intellectual framework that military professionalism demands.

Beyond the immediate aspects of the discussions, Hamdani displayed a lively sense of humor, a cosmopolitan attitude, and a clear understanding of the military events that extended well beyond his immediate level of experience and the sometimes bizarre nature of Saddam's regime.

It was clear in the interviews that while Hamdani did not speak English with any fluency, he could read English with considerable comprehension.[4] The entire research team found it a pleasure to talk honestly with an individual who has thought long and hard about his military experiences in the wars in which he participated and which have had such a catastrophic impact on his nation.

Topics of the discussions themselves ranged from the immediate tactical outcomes of particular actions in the Iran-Iraq War, to the interplay between the requirements of tyrannies (religious as well as secular) to control their political future, to the demands of military organizations for professionally competent officers who understand tactics and operations and who are able and willing to provide honest judgments of what is happening or might happen on the battlefield. In that respect, Ayatollah Ruhollah Khomeini's Iran and Saddam's Iraq exhibited considerable similarities, although Saddam at times proved a faster learner—at least over the course of his war against Iran. On the opposite side, Khomeini and his fellow religious leaders appear to have clung, right through to the conflict's end, to their belief that religious fanaticism and revolutionary spirit would triumph over all.

General Hamdani on several occasions commented on how much the American military had impressed him in both 1990 and 2003. Particularly interesting was his view that the U.S. Army was far superior to any he had seen in the Middle East—including the Israel Defense Forces. What particularly impressed him in 1990 was the sight of U.S. Soldiers along the Saudi-Kuwaiti border in full body armor and Kevlar helmets during the early period of Operation *Desert Shield*, despite the fact that the temperature was over 100 degrees and that hostilities had yet to begin. He claimed to have noted to one of his subordinates at the time that the American appearance alone underlined "a real sense of discipline."

The formal discussions documented in Part Two took place over a 4-day period in May 2007. Kevin Woods and Williamson Murray did most of the questioning, while Tom Holaday entered the discussions freely—sometimes in Arabic, sometimes in English. The relaxed nature under which the discussions took place allowed for maximum exchange of ideas and for follow-on questions to elucidate the matters under discussion.

The Arab-Israeli Wars and the Rise of the Ba'ath Party

Some of the most interesting and insightful discussions began with an examination of Hamdani's early military career before the Ba'ath party assumed full control of Iraq and its military organizations. General Hamdani entered the Iraqi army immediately after the 1967 Six-Day War had seen the Israeli ground and air forces completely shatter the military forces of Syria, Egypt, and Jordan in a blitz-krieg campaign that lasted less than a week.

He suggested that the humiliation of 1967 helped create not only the revolutionary political situation in Iraq (and other Arab nations) that brought the Ba'ath to power, but also a seriousness, purposefulness, and professionalism in the Iraqi army that had not existed before. That increased level of professionalism helps explain improvements in the fighting abilities those armies displayed in the 1973 Arab-Israeli War.[5] Arab armies, including Iraq's, took hard, realistic training far more seriously than they did before the Six-Day War. They also studied their Israeli enemy much more carefully. Thus, by the fall of 1973, the Iraqi army was tactically and logistically ready to deploy directly from Baghdad to fight on the Golan in the last battles of the war with surprising effectiveness. Concerning his knowledge of the enemy, Hamdani commented that even as a first lieutenant, he and many of his fellow junior officers knew the names and reputations of nearly every prominent Israeli general officer.

General Hamdani participated in the 1973 fighting on the Golan as a young company grade officer. The Iraqis, he claimed, were able to play an important role in the conflict by attacking the flank of the Israelis' two-division drive on Damascus. Whether the Israelis actually were going that far is another matter. Histories of the war suggest that the Iraqi attack persuaded the Israelis to halt their advance and move to reinforce the war's southern front, where the Egyptians were about to attempt their breakout from positions on the east bank of the Suez Canal. What was particularly interesting about Hamdani's comments was his contention that the 1973 war represented a significant high point of Iraqi military professionalism. The logistical movement from Iraq to the Golan, followed by the almost immediate conduct of operations by the Iraqis after they arrived at the battlefront during the heaviest fighting on the Golan Heights, became a standard to study and emulate in the Iraqi army.

Between the 1973 War and the Iran-Iraq War (1980–1988)

In the immediate aftermath of the 1973 Arab-Israeli War, the Iraqis continued their efforts to improve the army's overall level of professionalism and preparedness. General Hamdani claimed that the Iraqi army, still not overwhelmed by Ba'ath party "political correctness," carried out a careful analysis of the lessons from the Arab-Israeli War. A number of items still stuck in his mind from that effort. One lesson was that the Arab armies suffered from a considerable deficiency in technological knowledge—a direct result of the deficiencies in the educational systems of the Arab world—in comparison to their Israeli counterparts.

It was also clear to Hamdani that the Arab armies had largely modeled themselves—not surprisingly, given their origins in the colonial period—on the slow and methodical approach to war taken by the British Army. In contrast, the Israelis had modeled themselves on the Wehrmacht with its emphasis on speed, maneuver, decentralized leadership, and risk taking. The results of these educational and cultural differences showed clearly in the fighting on the Golan, where the Israelis reacted faster and adapted more quickly at the lower tactical levels than did their Arab opponents. These cultural and educational weaknesses would have little impact in the war with Iran, but they certainly influenced Iraqi performance in the two wars against U.S.-led coalitions.

General Hamdani admitted there were serious problems with the level of professionalism of his fellow officers in the Iraqi army (and other Arab armies, for that matter). Most displayed considerable disinterest in military history or how other military organizations (non-Arab) might operate. This dichotomy between Hamdani's ideal of what military professionalism should be and the reality of the Iraqi army only grew as the influence of Saddam and the Ba'ath party expanded during the course of Hamdani's military career.

Following the 1973 war, the Ba'ath began to make inroads into the army's professionalism. The party's leaders and senior military increasingly emphasized political loyalty and ideology as important elements in judging an officer's fitness for promotion. Saddam's seizure of power in 1979 further accelerated the politicization of the army. Whereas the saying in the early part of the Ba'ath rule had been "better a good soldier than a good Ba'athist," it changed to "better a good Ba'athist than a good soldier." The emphasis was now on political reliability and unquestioned obedience to orders rather than on serious military professionalism. Moreover, once firmly in charge, Saddam acted to promote a number of lieutenant colonels to major general, and subsequently to the command of divisions, without requiring them to hold any of the traditional staff or intermediate level command positions. Not surprisingly, this had a serious impact on the army's overall military effectiveness in a war with a much larger neighbor.

Not all of these officers were political puppets of the political elite; some were competent, serious officers. But Saddam had promoted them solely based on what he regarded as their political loyalty. Most crucially, from Hamdani's point of view, they had not commanded either battalions or brigades to provide a solid basis of military experience. Many had not even studied the profession of arms through attendance at the staff college, which might have at least equipped them intellectually to handle larger commands. In other words, they were not ready for either division or corps command.

Despite Ba'ath interference, however, the efforts made to improve the professionalism of the Iraqi army in the aftermath of the 1967 and 1973 defeats did play a significant role in the initial successes Iraq achieved against the Iranians in the early months of their conflict. But the larger problem that confronted the Iraqi military was the fact that its political masters, as well as its senior leaders, had no clear strategic or operational goals in mind for the upcoming war.[6]

The Iran-Iraq War (1980–1988)

Neither the Iraqis nor the Iranians prepared their forces for the war their political masters were spoiling for. At the beginning of the conflict, the leaders of the opposing sides had no clear understanding of the requirements for military effectiveness, or the difficulties their states would confront. Their feeling was that any sufficiently loyal politician or religious leader was capable of exercising effective military command—a belief for which their armies would pay a heavy price in lives and treasure. As the war continued, the armed forces of Iraq and Iran found themselves involved in desperate efforts to learn and adapt under pressures that threatened, at times, to overwhelm them. Tragically, it seems that in both nations, the obdurate ignorance of the political leadership would substantially retard the effort of military professionals to learn and adapt to the realities of the battlefield. Both national leaders (Saddam Hussein and Ayatollah Khomeini) significantly underestimated their opponent for similar reasons: both had little understanding of the limitations of their military institutions and even less understanding of their opponent.

Saddam believed that military effectiveness was a matter of the "warrior"—much as in medieval terms—and the spirit and morale of soldiers, not necessarily of training, organization, or discipline. To him bravery on the battlefield, exemplified by his personal vision of the Arab fighter, was the only reasonable measure of military effectiveness. As Hamdani mentioned in reference to Saddam's later confrontations with the Americans, the dictator could not grasp the significance of the scale and technological superiority of the American military.

Khomeini, on the other hand, equated military effectiveness on the battlefield with religious fanaticism. One of the measures of effectiveness both the Ayatollah and Saddam used to judge the effectiveness of their battlefield commanders was the relative number of casualties their troops suffered in battle—very much a World War I approach.[7] Early in the war, use of this metric was particularly true in the Iraqi case, as applied to division and corps commanders.

From Saddam's point of view, the fall of Shah Mohammed Reza Pahlavi and the political chaos engendered by Khomeini's religious revolution provided a perfect opportunity for him to act against Iran. Moreover, a number of Iraq's senior officers (some, but not all, recently appointed to their senior positions by Saddam) believed that the apparent collapse of the Shah's army meant there would be easy pickings to the east. What was not clear at the time, at least at Hamdani's level, was what exactly Saddam hoped to gain from a war against Iran, except perhaps the prestige of a "victory against the Persians."[8]

In hindsight, there appear to have been two political motives for Saddam's decision to go to war: first, to overturn the unfavorable 1975 treaty Iraq had signed with the Shah that dealt with the shared waterway to the Persian Gulf; second, and more important, to achieve victory over the Persians—at a cheap price—therefore legitimizing Iraq's claim that it deserved to replace Egypt as the head of the pan-Arab movement. This second motivation followed the "traitorous act" of Anwar Sadat, who, in signing the Camp David accords with Israel, had taken Egypt out of the so-called rejectionist camp. In other words, Saddam was aiming to assume Egyptian President Gamal Abdel-Nassir's mantle from the disgraced Sadat.

According to Hamdani, the Iraqis had no real military campaign plan in terms of operational objectives, or even coordinated tactical ones. Saddam appears to have believed that the invasion would quickly lead to Khomeini's fall and replacement by a regime that would surrender much of southwestern Iran to the Iraqis. Thus, the initial Iraqi operation was a thrust into southwestern Iran, which militarily achieved little except for the gaining of indefensible territory.

The major problem, however, lay in the fact that Saddam's leadership style had so politicized the army's senior levels that few, if any, generals were able, much less willing, to provide the dictator with honest assessments of the actual situation. Early in the conflict, "yes men" so dominated the Ba'athist regime's military decisionmaking processes at every level that only major defeats were going to alter the picture. Deployed into the territory seized from the Iranians, the Iraqi army was unprepared for the initial onslaught of the Iranians. Many of these attacks depended on religious fanaticism alone for success. Meanwhile, given the optimistic reports he was receiving from senior commanders, Saddam remained ignorant of the tactical vulnerabilities of his forces.

As Hamdani made clear, the only sensible operational approach that Saddam could have followed would have been to seize and then defend the passes leading out of Iran toward Iraq (predominantly in the central and northern sectors), as well as those in the Zagros Mountains through which Iranian forces would have had to deploy from the center of the country. This would have complicated Iranian efforts to launch and support their military forces against the Iraqis. But such a decision would have had to rest on Saddam's recognizing that a conflict with Iran was likely to be a long one—something he never foresaw. Consequently, the geographic positioning of the Iraqi army on key and defensible terrain was never seriously considered. Such an approach was not in the cards for a regime that consistently based its decisions on the dictator's ill-founded assumptions and hopes. Much as he would throughout his reign, Saddam tended to believe his own propaganda—war against Khomeini's Islamic Republic would prove an easy matter and would result in a glorious and quick victory.

On the other side of the hill, the chaos of the revolution meant that there were no coherent decisionmaking processes at all. Khomeini seemed to regard the conflict with Iraq as a God-given opportunity to solidify the revolution and defeat his political opponents in Tehran. Moreover, it also represented an opportunity to gain revenge for what he regarded as the ill treatment he had received at the hands of Saddam's government when, at the Shah's behest, it forced him in the mid-1970s to flee Iraq for Paris. It appears that Khomeini and his inner circle had even less understanding of military realities than Saddam.

According to Hamdani, undergirding Khomeini's passion for the war was a belief that religious fanaticism, reinforced by Persian nationalism, could overwhelm everything in its path. As a result, and almost until the bitter end, Khomeini would prove unwilling to make peace with Iraq short of complete victory. Iran would not back down, no matter how costly the war might become, at least until the point where its forces suffered a catastrophic series of military defeats—an unlikely event for a considerable time, given the preparation of Iraq's military for a major conflict. Thus, while Saddam was looking for a cheap, easy victory, the Persians were looking to accomplish the complete overthrow of Saddam's regime and its replacement by a Shia puppet regime.[9]

The Iranian military had a number of serious problems. Foremost was the fact that the revolution caused deep fractures within Iranian society—fractures that represented contending political and religious factions, as well as the divided nature of opposition to the Shah's regime. Iran's military already had been purged of those loyal to the Shah or those whom the new regime did not trust. Even after the purges, the Iranian military had little standing with those in the political realm. Military professionalism was simply not in the vocabulary of Khomeini's regime. The alternative to the professional military in Iran was a number of revolutionary militias. None of these militias had any serious military training, nor, as Hamdani would describe, did they possess leaders with even the slightest understanding of tactics.

The militias—in some cases no more than small groups swearing fealty to a local imam or ayatollah with political ambitions—often acted independently, obeying no instructions and initiating combat actions without orders to do so. Local Iranian commanders appeared to have had almost complete freedom of action, whatever the strategic or operational consequences might be. This may well explain the fact that some Iranian units began shelling Iraqi towns and military positions in a rampageous fashion before the Iraqi invasion began and before the initiation of large-scale military operations. Thus, one can hardly speak of coherent Iranian military operations, much less a strategic conception, throughout the first 4 years of the conflict.

While the militias were important in the dangerous game of politics swirling around Tehran, they had no military training and remained disjointed, answering to different clerics and factions among Khomeini's supporters and exhibiting little interest in repairing their military deficiencies. Not surprisingly, their attitudes reflected those of their leaders, and they showed little or no willingness to learn from, much less cooperate in military operations with, the regular army. All of this derived from their belief that religious fervor was the key to victory on the battlefield. Thus, Iranian tactics remained unimaginative and militarily incompetent throughout the war. More often than not, human wave attacks were all the Iranian militias could launch. The result was a catastrophic casualty tally reminiscent of the fighting in World War I.

Unlike in Baghdad, where Saddam attempted to control everything, the exact opposite military command model was in effect in Tehran. Various factional leaders, imams, and others launched attacks or raids in an effort to curry favor with the religious and political leaders, who were in turn jockeying for position around Khomeini. Early in the war, few if any of Iran's attacks appeared to have coherence or clear objectives, nor did they fit into a larger strategic conception of the war. Most battles thus contributed to the growing casualties while achieving little of tactical, much less operational, value. This situation reflected the general lack of military understanding among the religious and political leaders in Tehran, who were supposedly running the show.

The War's Course

According to Hamdani, the first 3 years of the conflict reflected the miscalculations of the opposing sides. Once embarked upon, the war absorbed the attention of those fighting, while desperate attempts to mobilize larger forces sapped the ability to adapt and change in a coherent fashion. Saddam's top-down interference and lack of understanding of military realities led the Iraqi army to carry out a series of ill-conceived movements that, despite leading to the capture of Khorramshahr, were without clear objectives.[10] The war itself began with bombardments on both sides that reflected the war of words surging between Tehran and Baghdad. While Iranian troops fought with considerable fanaticism at the local level, they displayed no coherent or effective response to the initial Iraqi moves. The battle of Khorramshahr (October 6–24, 1980) proved to be a violent and bloody affair in which each side suffered around 7,000 casualties. Eventually Iraqi firepower and tactical superiority took the remains of what had once been a city.

In analyzing Iranian military operations in the first months of the conflict, Hamdani suggested that no one appeared to be in charge on the Iranian side. Instead, local regular army and militia commanders, supported by mullahs on the scene (who played an analogous role to that of commissars in the Red Army during World War II), responded to Iraqi moves as they saw fit, with little or no coordination with each other or the national authorities. Many in Tehran seemed content simply to beat the drum of fanatical religious propaganda. Others provided irrelevant advice, based on their misconceptions and faulty assumptions. New units arriving at the front had little coherent or sensible training, nor for a considerable period did there appear to be any kind of lessons-learned process among the units of Iran's various military forces. Thus, little combat learning took place among Iranian forces over the first several years of the war.

Khomeini responded to initial Iraqi incursions with a massive mobilization of Iran, which provided huge numbers of men for the militias—and fewer for the army—who were willing to die as martyrs. Iran, with its far larger population, enjoyed a significant advantage over Iraq in this regard. Nevertheless, Khomeini never seems to have understood the need for military professionalism. Throughout the war with Iraq, Iran's senior leaders harbored suspicion of those officers from the Shah's army who survived the early purges. Hamdani recalled that according to captured Iranian officers, the evaluation of military competence largely rested on a judgment as to how religious a commander was or was not. Moreover, the heads of the various militias displayed little or no interest in exploiting the expertise of the regular officers for the training of their units.

Ironically, with the massive mobilization, the threat that Khomeini represented to the stability of the oil regions of the Middle East made it difficult for the Iranians to acquire the heavy weapons such as tanks or new aircraft that played a key part in the fighting on the ground. It also led to a situation where the Iraqis—with access to modern Soviet and Western weapons—were able to increase their technological capabilities slowly but steadily. According to Hamdani, the result of Iran's lack of access to sophisticated modern weapons was that, as they depleted the stock of heavy weapons and spares acquired by the Shah, they had to field a light infantry force supported by diminishing amounts of armor and artillery. This was not necessarily a disadvantage in swampy areas like the Fao Peninsula or the mountains to the northeast of Baghdad, but it put the Iranians at a distinct disadvantage in areas of flat desert terrain and at the approaches to Basra, where much of the heavy fighting occurred.

After the initial advance into Iran, many of the Iraqi generals deployed at the front failed to meet the challenge of complex operations. Moreover, in Hamdani's opinion, their lack of experience led to inferiority complexes and made them unwilling to take advice from their subordinates. The result was a series of stunning defeats, beginning in 1981, that drove the Iraqis back to and then beyond the starting point of their invasion.[11] These defeats forced Saddam to move gradually away from his emphasis on political reliability for his generals toward greater willingness to reward and promote those who displayed some level of military competence. Still, as Hamdani emphasized during our conversations, Saddam never let go of his deep suspicion of his generals and his belief that they represented the only potentially serious threat to his dictatorship.

By mid-1982, the Iraqis managed to stabilize the military situation back on their own territory. Hamdani indicated that special operations forces, combined with armored support, played a major role in bringing this about. However, Iraq's special forces proved a wasting asset and by the end of 1982 had been almost completely exhausted by the heavy losses suffered through continuous use. Despite its success, there would be few attempts to rebuild Iraqi special forces over the remainder of the conflict. The high casualty rates of junior officers at the front and the expansion of the Iraqi army meant that both the quantity and quality of officers qualified for special operations duty dropped as the war spun out of control.

The War of Attrition: 1982–1985

The military and strategic situation forced Saddam in 1982 to begin the mass mobilization of the Iraqi nation. By that point, he realized he had involved Iraq in a long war and that no easy or quick solutions would bring peace. In that year, he created the Republican Guard to provide his commanders with greater flexibility in responding to the constant series of Iranian offensives. The Republican Guard was to form a counterattack force against the major Iranian offensives, which marked much of the fighting throughout this period. Those Iranian offensives, beginning in the summer of 1982, swept like an arc around Basra from north to south as the Iranians groped for weaknesses in the Iraqi defenses. The Iranian efforts in the south—their main emphasis throughout the entire war—reflected their hope that the Shia of the region would respond to their coreligionists from Iran (which they did not).[12] Nevertheless, these Iranian offensive operations put immense pressure on the Iraqi forces.

The fact that Khomeini's military forces, both the regular army and the militia, were increasingly becoming an all-infantry army that relied almost entirely on human wave attacks had a considerable effect on the fighting. The lack of armor and artillery limited the pressure Iranians could put on the Iraqis on the northern front, because while the mountainous terrain on the border favored infantry operations, the more open terrain lying beyond provided Iraqi armor with an enormous advantage, of which it made full use. Similar factors held in the south, where swamps and waterlogged terrain helped the Iranians to the east of Basra, but the more open and urban terrain around Basra and to the west favored the Iraqis.

By this point in the war, the heavy losses in the initial fighting had severely depleted the Iraqi officer corps, which never fully recovered despite Saddam's mobilization efforts. Still, the Iraqis were able to mobilize sufficient forces to halt the Iranians and begin a dogged defense of the territory—and oil wells—near Basra and the mountainous approaches to the east of Baghdad.

Throughout this period, the opposing sides had to resort to a war of attrition. The Iranians consistently used human wave attacks aimed at overwhelming

Iraqi positions and imposing heavy casualties on the defenders. On the Iraqi side, there was little thought given to major counterattacks, except where important positions had fallen. Rather, the goal was to inflict as many casualties as possible on the attackers. The Iraqis (particularly Saddam) saw hope in the situation, believing that in view of their terrible losses, the Iranians would eventually overthrow Khomeini and agree to a ceasefire.

In 1983, having had little success in their attacks against Basra's defenses, the Iranians opened a major offensive against the approaches to Baghdad through the mountains northeast of the capital. Their aim, according to Hamdani, was to establish a second front against the Iraqis in an area where they could gain substantial aid from the locals.[13] In this case, the Kurds—to Saddam's fury—broke the truce they had agreed to and cooperated with the Iranian attacks.[14] It also appears that Khomeini was putting substantial pressure on his military commanders to achieve a major success similar to that of the 1981 counterattack against Saddam.

The Iranian offensive foundered for two reasons. First was the Iranians' inability to move beyond the tactical mode and articulate a level of operational capability to exploit tactical successes when they occurred. The cause of this failure was a general lack of professionalism at the higher levels of Iranian military forces—not surprising when ayatollahs appeared to play as much of a (if not the dominant) role as senior Iranian officers in decisionmaking. The second reason pertained to the fact that the Iraqis, possessing what to all intents and purposes were interior lines, could shuffle divisions quickly from the south, where they had concentrated most of their strength to meet the Iranian offensives, to the north. Moreover, the Iraqis at the highest levels were beginning to exhibit some awareness of how to operate at the operational level of war.

As their losses mounted at the lower tactical level, the Iranians became increasingly proficient at infiltration and small unit tactics. In this arena, they were clearly superior to their opponents. Thus, in mountainous terrain east of Baghdad, in the north, and in the swampy terrain characterizing the areas to the northeast and southeast of Basra, they enjoyed considerable advantage. But elsewhere, where the ground lay open and thus amenable to the use of armor, Iraq's superior armored forces, backed by dug-in infantry and artillery, halted enemy attacks and inflicted disproportionate casualties on the attacking Iranians. As a result, the war took on the guise of World War I attrition, as the two sides' military forces, equipped and trained in different patterns, inflicted heavy casualties on each other without being able to gain a decisive advantage. By 1984, however, the Iraqis began to use chemical weapons, which did provide them an important advantage, given the failure of the Iranians to prepare for such a threat. The use of these weapons would continue for the remainder of the war.[15]

It was during this portion of the war that Hamdani received his most dangerous assignment. At the time, he was a battalion commander, having reached that rank largely on the basis of his military competence and the incompetence of others, rather than his penchant for suggesting new ideas to his superiors. He received Saddam's two sons—as well as Tariq Aziz's son—to serve as officers in his battalion. Saddam's propaganda message was that even his sons were serving in combat, so all of Iraq's people must participate in the war for what was clearly the survival of the Ba'ath regime. However, Saddam provided Hamdani with more nuanced instructions: he was to ensure that neither son fell into Iranian hands or, by implication, died in battle. General Hamdani suggested that his success in this task could be one of the only reasons he remains alive today. The close relation he established with Qusay, Saddam's heir apparent, probably kept him out of prison in the mid-1990s and saved his career after he dared to offer military suggestions that contradicted Saddam's views.

1986 and After

The Iranians did display some ability to learn. In 1986, they launched an offensive against the Fao Peninsula southeast of Basra. Catching the Iraqis off guard, they seized the peninsula with a joint amphibious assault heavily supported by artillery. The Iraqi defenders, coordinated from Baghdad, expected an attack on Basra from the northeast and were completely unprepared for the Iranian strike at Fao. Moreover, they failed to react quickly, which magnified the Iranian success. In the marshes and canals of the Fao Peninsula, Iraqi tanks proved vulnerable because of their lack of maneuverability. Not surprisingly, the Iraqi counterattacks were a complete failure.

In the Fao campaign, for the first time since the war began, Iranians displayed a significant degree of military professionalism. They made every effort to play to their strengths while minimizing those of the Iraqis. They launched major forces against the swampy terrain that makes up most of the peninsula. For the attack, they trained a large force of infantry for an amphibious assault and prepared large numbers of small boats and landing craft. The infantry infiltration tactics they had developed on the central sector played to the geographic realities of the swamps on the peninsula. According to Hamdani, the North Koreans provided sophisticated combat engineering advice and support to Khomeini's forces. Perhaps most significantly, the Iranians managed to achieve a modicum of cooperation between the remnants of the regular army and the various militias. This allowed them to plan the operation over the winter of 1985/1986 with considerable precision.

Iraqi overconfidence, together with the unwillingness of those in Baghdad to recognize what was happening, served to magnify the initial Iranian successes. The commanders on the spot showed a distinct bravado that they could halt any Iranian attack, while commanders at higher levels in the Basra area displayed a lack of imagination in analyzing what the Iranians were up to. Extensive radio deception by the Iranians played a role in convincing the Iraqis by reinforcing their prejudices and assumptions. When the Iraqi generals in the area finally realized that something major was occurring on the peninsula, senior military and political leaders in Baghdad further delayed in sending reinforcements, because they concluded that the Iranians were staging a deception operation and that their main attack would come against Basra. Not until Iraqi forces—approximately of division strength—had been crushed and had lost most of the Fao Peninsula did commanders in Basra and Baghdad awaken to the danger. By then it was too late.

The hesitation to reinforce those units defending the peninsula, particularly the 26th Division, which were under enormous pressure and on the brink of collapse, appears to have stemmed from fear that the Iranians would launch a major offensive against Baghdad, the loss of which would mean the end of Saddam's regime. Hurried reinforcements arrived into a chaotic situation. The Iraqi army responded with counterattacks by heavy armored units. In the bogs and swamps of the Fao Peninsula, this poorly coordinated approach of armored forces made no sense; it played into the hands of the Iranian forces' strengths and resulted only in heavy losses of men and equipment without regaining any significant territory. It was a sobering experience for all involved.

It is now apparent that the Iranian strike against the Fao Peninsula was the opening move of a major offensive to seize Basra and deal the Ba'athist regime an immense military and political blow. The initial Basra attacks failed, but the commanders of the III and VII Corps, close associates of Saddam, were political generals and consistently overstated the losses their troops were inflicting on the Iranians.[16] Thus, when a further wave of even larger Iranian attacks hit Iraqi positions, the Iraqis were clearly in danger of losing Basra and the oil wells to the west. They held on, but largely due to Iranian mistakes and the enemy's inability to exploit any of the gains and breakthroughs its attacking forces had made.

The situation around Basra was desperate and remained so for much of the rest of the year. General Hamdani described the fighting as another "Battle of the Somme," in which both sides suffered extraordinarily heavy losses. The number of Iraqis killed in action approached 50,000; Iran's losses were two to three times higher—at least by Hamdani's estimate. In the end, the Iraqis held back the Iranian tide. Chemical weapons played a major role, as did the failure of the Iranians to prepare their forces to deal with such weapons.

Recovery from the Defeat on the Fao Peninsula

The fighting around Basra did prove a sobering experience for Saddam, who finally, at least in this conflict, placed more trust in military professionals. Certainly, the difficulties the Iraqis encountered in defending Basra after the defeat on the Fao Peninsula were considerable impetus for the increased interest in professionalism for the short term. In fact, throughout 1986, the Iraqis carried out a number of reforms at all levels that were to have a substantial impact not only on the defensive battles of 1987, but also the devastating counterattacks they launched in 1988, which finally broke the back of Iran's—and Khomeini's—willingness to continue the conflict.

The most important reform in Iraq came in July 1986. Saddam made the decision to pull the Republican Guard units out of the front line and begin a wholesale reequipping and retraining effort from squad level all the way to division and corps command. This involved the arrival of the most modern Soviet tanks and armored personnel carriers called BMPs (*boyevaya mashina pekhoty,* or infantry fighting vehicle) as well as heavy artillery. Saddam seems to have recognized that he needed to make a major effort to improve Iraq's military capabilities or face defeat. Thus, there was a greater willingness at the top to pay serious attention to the recommendations of the more professional officers to build up the Republican Guard's capabilities. In addition, Saddam authorized major recruiting drives among those who had largely avoided military service thus far in the conflict. Targeted were students, the sons of tribal leaders, and many of the wealthier classes. In particular, the recruiting effort targeted Anbar Province, one of the strongholds of Sunni and Ba'athist support for Saddam, which was to gain the distinction of being the only province in Iraq not to revolt during the troubles in 1991.

This effort to improve the combat effectiveness of the Republican Guard involved more extensive training at all levels to improve tactical and battlefield proficiency of officers commanding Republican Guard units. Initially, the aim was to create a force that could dominate the battlefield by counterattacking Iranian infantry penetrations of Iraqi defensive positions. Saddam initially hoped to create 10 divisions for this purpose, but the Iraqis were ultimately able to create only 5. One constraint was the inability to fill the critical officer positions owing to the loss of so many competent junior officers during the war's first 6 years.

Saddam's son-in-law, Hussein Kamel, was in charge of the overall effort to improve the Republican Guard.[17] Perhaps as a result of his limited military qualifications, Kamel proved willing to listen to the more competent Republican Guard staff officers and commanders, the most important of whom was Ayad Al-Rawi. The problem remained that a substantial number of Republican Guard commanders were brave but professionally unprepared and often incompetent in the positions they held. Overall, however, by 1987, the Iraqis were able to field a number of relatively effective Republican Guard units—at least in comparison to the Iraqi and Iranian units that had fought the war thus far. These Republican Guards were to play a crucial role in the last 2 years of the conflict.

In the fighting that occurred in 1987—almost all of it around Basra—the newly refurbished and expanded Republican Guard divisions proved to be the decisive force Saddam had been in search of since 1980. The Iranians continued their major attacks aimed at taking Basra, during which they again showed little willingness to learn from previous experiences. Moreover, much of the religious fanaticism that had characterized their troops in the war thus far began to subside. Given the huge losses the forces had suffered without discernable gains, the Iranian leaders, political as well as military, were beginning to have difficulty motivating their soldiers.

However, the major factor in the Iraqi ability to hold off the Iranian attacks lay in the skill and capabilities of the expanded and improved Republican Guard formations. In the heavy fighting throughout 1987 just to the east and northeast of Basra, Republican Guard units repeatedly hammered the Iranian breakthroughs and quickly retook the ground the Iranians seized. The continued success of these counterattacks had the effect of steadily lowering Iranian morale and setting the stage for the major Iraqi offensive of 1988.

The Iraqi offensive for 1988 aimed to regain the territory lost to the Iranians on the Fao Peninsula. Planning began relatively early in 1988 and involved Saddam and six senior officers. Not until immediately before the offensive were the staffs brought into the planning processes. Beyond the six officers and Saddam, no one knew the extent of the coming offensive. The attack had major political as well as operational goals, because the loss of the Fao Peninsula, the one success the Iranians had enjoyed thus far in the war, would deal Khomeini's regime a major blow.

Deception operations covered the Iraqi preparations for the offensive. It is still not clear what happened on the other side, but Iranian intelligence appears to have missed the signs of the impending Iraqi attack. The Republican Guard's offensive caught the Iranians flat-footed. Whatever improvements had occurred in their military forces—substantially less than those of Iraq—major rifts remained between the militias and the regular army and among the militias themselves. The Iranians reacted not at all at first, a fact that probably reflected the same overly optimistic reporting to Tehran by senior commanders at the front that had marked the Iraqi reporting about the Iranian attack on the Fao Peninsula in 1986. The slow reporting exacerbated the fact that Iranian forces possessed relatively little mobility and, hence, found it difficult to react effectively to a deteriorating situation.

Once again, the Iraqi attack resembled a World War I offensive with its heavy emphasis on the use of artillery and gas against the Iranians. By catching Khomeini's forces by surprise, the Iraqis were able to minimize their weakness in command and control (C^2)—a weakness on both sides throughout the war—while maximizing the C^2 difficulties on the other side.[18] Most of the Iranians fought doggedly, but the surprise the Iraqis had gained, as well as careful planning and preparation for the battle, allowed the Republican Guard to dominate the battlefield even considering the difficulties of the terrain. Firepower, gas, and superior planning eventually resulted in a devastating defeat for the Iranians. Shortly thereafter, Khomeini agreed to an armistice with Saddam's Ba'athist regime, and the dismal Iran-Iraq War came to an end.

Thoughts on the Iran-Iraq "Cold-War" in the 1990s

General Hamdani offered some interesting observations on what the Iraqis believed they confronted in terms of an Iranian threat in the 1990s. Historically, Iraq has been the borderland between the Arab and Persian worlds, with major Iranian invasions in 1626 and 1754 of the Mesopotamian valley, then held by the Ottoman empire. He emphasized the historical Iranian drive to the west in both military and cultural terms.[19] Saddam's initial response to the Iranian problem in the postwar period was to emphasize the naval and air components of a future conflict—clearly an indication that even he had been influenced by the cost of the ground fighting.[20] Included in his analysis was an emphasis on mobile ballistic missiles, which had played a major role in what the Iraqis had termed "the Battle of the Cities."[21]

From what the Iraqis could tell, the Iranians made major efforts throughout the period to bring their military forces up to the standards set by the Iraqis in the last year of the war. The shambles that the Americans had made of Iraq's military in the 1991 Gulf War also played a role in these Iranian efforts. There did appear to be considerable efforts to bring the Pasdaran and Quds militias up to some semblance of professional standards. The events of 1990–1991 had a huge impact on the Iraqi military, while the continued confrontation with the United States during the 1990s made it difficult to focus on the Iranian threat.

Still, Saddam and most officers believed that a renewed war with the Iranians was more likely than another major conflict with the United States. Given the experiences of 1980–1988, however, most felt such a conflict would not involve a similar conventional war, but rather Iranian efforts to infiltrate agents, arms, and small forces to support another major rebellion by the Shia.[22]

Comments on Saddam Hussein as Political and Military Leader

General Hamdani provided a detailed and nuanced view of Saddam as a military and political leader. He first noted that Saddam possessed a complex personality—"one could say that he possessed multiple personalities." The dictator was highly intelligent and, when open-minded, which he was at times, quick to grasp essential points. On the military side, his openness largely depended on the difficulties Iraqi forces were confronting at the time. In the early days of the war with Iran, for example, he was quite open and flexible when adapting to difficult military situations. For the most part, however, he tended to confuse reality with what he wished to be true.

Saddam was certainly not an easy person to explain. According to Hamdani, the dictator was a combination of Stalin, the ruthless ruler, and Hitler, the aspiring general. Interestingly, the first military uniform that Saddam put on was that of an Iraqi field marshal. Hamdani recalled that Saddam could in the blink of an eye switch between his various personalities: "In one moment…he might kill a member of his own family without a care; then the next moment he would be extremely sensitive, tears in his eyes over the injury of a cat." To make matters especially difficult for those who worked in his immediate surroundings or had to brief him, one never knew from moment to moment which one of Saddam's personalities was going to emerge.

Saddam had little understanding of military issues or what made for effectiveness in military institutions. Not only did he not want to know about the extent of American military and technological superiority, he also largely dismissed such factors as irrelevant on the battlefield. What mattered to him was the ideal of the Arab "warrior," an individual who, he believed, had consistently proved his superiority on the battlefields of history and who would do so again. Above all, Saddam had no understanding of strategy.

The military defeats and the serious operational situation at the front brought an increasing sense of military realism to Saddam's approach to the war with Iran. That was much less the case in 1990–1991 and no longer the case by 2003. The combat conditions of 1982–1984 forced him to give greater freedom to his subordinates and, for the most part, made him more receptive to their advice. Nevertheless, political loyalty to the Ba'ath regime and particularly to its president remained the foremost of his criteria for selecting senior officers.

Up to the Kuwait adventure, Saddam's focus was on being a strong leader. But after the disaster of Kuwait, there was a significant change in his personality. With the rebellion of March 1991, he lost his trust in the Iraqi people, and his paranoia deepened. From that point on, virtually every decision that he made appeared focused on maintaining his control over Iraq. Combined with his paranoia and lack of trust in nearly everybody, the result was an Iraq where practically no sensible decisions could be made. Moreover, everyone in his immediate circle, including his sons, was terrified to the point that few were willing to suggest anything that they thought might upset the dictator.

In the mid-1990s, his persona significantly changed—again for the worse. The defection of his son-in-law, Kamel, to Jordan affected him deeply. From Saddam's perspective, the worst had happened: a member of the Tikriti mafia—in fact, of his inner family—had betrayed him. As a result, he isolated himself from everyone. Rarely did he go out among the people. He no longer trusted his senior officers, and some of his senior ministers went up to 2 years without seeing him. Finally, he no longer visited or reviewed the Republican Guards. It was during this period that Saddam began the construction of great palaces all over Iraq, few of which he ever visited.

During this period of isolation, Saddam spent much of his time writing stories, poems, and novels. In 1995, he called his senior commanders, including all the division commanders, together. At the time, Saddam was holding an extended soirée with a group of artists and writers. The generals were held in expectation of the emergency meeting with Saddam and then were told to go home without ever having discussed anything with him. This last stage, which culminated in his unwillingness to address the increasing threat from the United States in 2002, was marked throughout by Saddam's thoroughly unrealistic expectations and his inability to connect reality with his own hopes and dreams.

Part Two.
The Interviews

The following transcripts are from a series of long conversations with General Ra'ad Hamdani on May 14–19, 2007, in Jordan. The conversations occurred predominantly in Arabic with a mix of simultaneous and parallel translation into English. Interview transcripts have been edited for clarity and readability. Project members (Kevin Woods, Williamson Murray, and Thomas Holaday) are identified by name in connection with the questions each asked.

Discussion One

Arab-Israeli Wars of 1967 and 1973 — Military Transition under Ba'athist Rule

Murray: Please allow me to frame my questions with a few guiding ideas. These questions derive from what American military historians have focused on for the last 20–30 years. First, we are beginning to understand that no matter how good an army is on the tactical and operational levels of war, if it doesn't get the strategy and politics right also, it loses. The crucial area is how well the strategy and the policy at the ends and means are calculated. Second, we understand that military organizations always get the "next war" wrong to one extent or another. The issue is how well prepared they are to adapt to the actual conditions of the war that confronts them. Finally, and mixed in with the processes of adaptation in a long war where both sides adapt, both sides change and so the critical element is to maintain that adaptation process throughout the course of the war. That said, many of our questions will focus on how well the Iraqi and Iranian military commanders at different levels adapted to the war they fought.

I'd like to begin by asking about your views on the 1973 Yom Kippur War, recognizing that you were a very junior officer at the time—my guess is that you understood a great deal of the things that happened then later on in your career. The Arab armies did substantially better in the 1973 war than they did in the 1967 war. Can you explain your perceptions of how such an improvement took place over such a relatively short time—between 1967 and 1973?

Hamdani: First of all, the loss in 1967 was a great disappointment for the Arab population because of the high expectations. It got to the point where people in most Arab countries rallied to demonstrate their dissatisfaction with the results of the war and even to ask for a change in the military leadership, and actually the current government at that time. So because of the disappointment that reigned over the Arab community, Arab political and military leaders made an effort to study the 1967 war and find lessons to be learned. This had a tremendous impact on the 1973 war.

Before 1967, the numbers of the military were very small, equipment was not up to date, and additionally, everyone in the community believed that just by having the Egyptian and the Syrian armies working together, they could actually get the job done against the Israelis. When that failed, the resulting shock led to a loss of confidence in the militaries and governments. Nassir's resignation was a direct result.[23]

There were similar movements in Syria, and even in Iraq, where the Ba'ath party made requests for the resignation of Abd al-Rahman Arif, since his government was unpopular and incapable of facing the challenge from Israel or any other potential adversary.[24] Then, the 1968 military coup took place in Iraq, partially justified on the setback caused by the defeat of 1967. One could see the effects in Egypt as well, where people started to despise the average Egyptian soldier and call him a "Deserter of Sinai."

You see, the shock experienced by the Arab people was equivalent to the shock of September 11, 2001, for Americans. You could multiply the dissatisfaction felt in America by 10 to understand the atmosphere in the Arab countries around Israel at the time. When the battle began, I was in my last year of high school taking the final exams, but the authorities canceled everything. Everyone was disappointed and crying because of the loss of 1967—it was the loss of an illusion about the strength of the Arab armies.

So based on this, officers began to study Arab military capabilities—in Egypt, Syria, and Iraq. They started to study the reasons for the Arab defeat and reassess the military capabilities of their own forces.

Murray: The Chinese military theorist Sun Tzu says that one of the most important elements in war is to know one's enemy. My sense is that in 1967, the Arab armies, both in terms of professional attitudes as well as popular attitudes, simply did not know or understand or even fear their enemy, whereas in 1973, there was a far more serious and professional understanding that they were up against very, very tough people.

Hamdani: Part of the answer lies in a different area—the old Arab military leadership after 1967 reassessed and reorganized the structure of their forces. Moreover, they reconsidered the political ideology and objectives of the armies— by that, I mean all armies including the Iraqi army. They realized through the assessments that most of the Arab forces had rested on the British model, while the Israeli forces were similar to the German model of World War II.

So we, as the Iraqi army, adopted a system called the "battle legion" that integrated infantry and armor. Before 1967, those two branches had trained to fight separately. After 1967, they merged to conduct combined arms operations for the infantry and the tanks. Furthermore, after that, the air forces were connected to the armored and infantry forces—thus, there was more cooperation. The air force's task had previously remained limited to support operations, but its aircraft now became integrated with ground operations. Because of this integration between the ground and air, we came to realize the importance of ground-based air defense systems. In previous years, we had used only the air force against the enemy's air force. Due to the reassessments and integration, we were able to create a form of joint air defense system. The air force realized that when it comes to air defense, it is not just the air force that has the job, but it must also come from the lower levels, from the infantrymen.

We requested a lot of information from the Soviet Union at that time, and many officers attended military planning sessions there and had Soviet experts visit Iraq to exchange ideas and train and support our forces.

The largest problem we encountered was the fact that the world was very advanced technologically, while the education level of the Arab soldier was at a very basic level. At that time, as young officers, we had a major responsibility, especially when we requested new equipment, mostly Soviet equipment. But even this new equipment was of lower quality than the equipment provided to the Israelis by the Americans. President [Lyndon B.] Johnson's granting of considerable supplies of U.S. weapons and equipment to Israel, such as the F–4 Phantom II, represented a terrifying level of support for us. In 1964, I remember seeing a video with President [John F.] Kennedy in it, where the Americans displayed a demonstration or training exercise with the Phantom aircraft dropping its bombs and firing missiles. This had a psychological impact on Arab officers, especially Iraqi officers, because that's the way they look at it—that's whom we fight, that's our enemy, and that's their capability. Therefore, they all felt afraid of the Phantom, which we knew and had seen in 1964, and which in 1969 went to the Israeli military, because of the American contribution to Israel. So our expectations of the enemy's capabilities were high.

It was clear that [Iraq] needed modern weapons and technology from the Soviet Union in order to counter those of the Israelis. But the real problem was that even if we had the equipment, we did not have the scientific expertise and training to actually make good use of it. This was the objective after 1967, to get revenge and regain respect for the Arab countries. This was accomplished, first of all, by changing the objectives, the mentality of the military leaders, as well as the style of how we fought during the first war.

I graduated from the military academy in 1967, in Jordan, and most of our topics of study, training, and combat exercises were about the geography and operational range of Israel. As a lieutenant, I had seven or eight books in my tent all about the Israeli training, preparations, and weapons, and the American weapons and so forth. Everybody was interested in learning about our enemy, learning about his capabilities, his ideology. Even from my tent I would watch and try to identify the different tanks and airplanes that I saw—seeing the French AMX–13 [tank], the Centurion [British tank], the Phantom [American fighter], the Sukhoi [Soviet fighter flown by Arab air forces], and the Mystère [French fighter]—this sort of thing to get more information and learn more about our enemy. I fully recognized that our competence is represented by how much we understand the enemy.

In 1972, the 71st Brigade moved from Jordan to Iraq, along with the rest of the 3^{d} Armored Division, which was the best division in the Iraqi army at that point. We adopted the same battle system as the Israeli army; we trained the same way, and we carried out several long maneuvers over months in the desert in southern Iraq, for any future involvement [in a confrontation with the Israelis]. We learned that one has to do rehearsals and exercises on a consistent and intense basis.

So in the 1973 confrontation, we had a much better understanding of the capability of our enemy; we knew largely what to expect. We had mainly focused on having the Israelis as our opponent. In 1967, we had the audacity, after putting all the Arab forces together, to ask, "Who is this Israeli force?" But in 1973, we needed to exact revenge on the Israelis—that was the objective, regardless of the cost. When the combat started in 1973, I was still a first lieutenant, but I was completely aware of the Israeli army's leadership—the names and backgrounds of its generals. This shows you how much interest in studying the enemy we had. We considered ourselves in 1973 to be in a position to challenge the Israeli army. [Moreover], we witnessed how even after their losses they were able to come back and balance, to rebalance their position after the initial Arab gains in the 1973 fighting.

Woods: Let me ask a follow-up question on the last point. The lessons of 1967 that affected 1973—comparing that short period of 6 years, where the Arab armies were able to learn and perform at a much higher level than they had in 1967, to the period right after 1973—raises interesting questions. Can you explain to me the lessons process after the 1973 war? In other words, what was the focus of the Arab armies (specifically the Iraqi army) after the 1973 war, as it unknowingly moved toward the Iran-Iraq War?

Hamdani: In the aftermath of the 1973 conflict, there was a feeling that Israel was becoming stronger than we could imagine. We thought that our preparations for 1973, all the assessments and the reorganizations of the Arab forces, would enable us to eliminate the Israeli army and force it to return to the [pre-1967] borders of Israel. But the results of the war gave us the impression that Israel was stronger than we could imagine—all of our preparations had still not [made us equal] to the effectiveness of the Israeli army. We learned that they were far more well equipped and trained than what we expected after the 1973 conflict. I joined the Iraqi Staff College in 1978 and graduated in 1980. All the exercises we studied, theoretically and on the maps, all of them related to Israel, and not on any other target, such as Iran. Another objective for Iraq was to determine how an army might push the Israeli army back to its original borders.

So there was hatred toward the United States of America because we felt that we were unable to defeat the Israelis because of the solid American support for them—which affected the political and psychological situation of the United States. After the war, especially from 1977 to 1979, Arab countries started to become more realistic militarily, when talking about the Israeli forces and their capabilities.

We also talked about the normalization of relations between the biggest Arab country, Egypt, and Israelis in the Camp David Agreement.[25] After this, a fissure emerged between the realistic politics of many Arab political leaders and the emotions of the Arab people toward Israel. The trust between the people and the political leaderships collapsed. This split also occurred between Iraq and Egypt. Iraq was trying to maintain the [split as an] issue and embarrass the Egyptian leadership for its peace projects with Israel. So there was a split between the political leaderships of Iraq and most other Arab countries, and the Arab people. This affected the position of the army and its preparations.

For the first time it became apparent that there was a big difference between the political theories (or ideologies) and the reality of the political situation. Therefore, our generation of captains and majors felt that we were going to coordinate the units—the combat unit leaderships, because we were the ones about to take command. We sensed a reality not consistent with the direction of most Arab leaders. A new school started [within the Iraqi officer corps] that we called the "reality school." We began to differentiate between our real leaders, who were wise in thinking and speaking, and those who just held high ranks but were weak thinkers. It motivated me to become the sort of effective leader who used his brain to understand the processes [involved in] any potential conflict.

The political change in Iraq, of changing the direction of our military, did not begin until 1979–1980.[26] We actually had a full armored corps ready to go into combat at a high level with the Israeli forces. Our thoughts and sights always focused toward the west. So making the switch of the objectives, goals, and targets from the west to the east represented a dramatic change within the military community. Our great experience, exercises, and previous engagements with the Israelis led to our initial and relatively quick success over Iranian forces in the early stages of the war. That is, our confrontations with the Israeli forces and preparations for the next war with them pressured a rather unsophisticated army to become a well-trained one with different people and a different ideology—it helped the professionalizing processes in the Iraqi army.

Murray: In terms of 1973, this was the one war where Arab strategy connected with the actual means and ends available, and where the politicians reduced their interference, at least in terms of the actual conduct of military operations. This gave the maximum authority to military professionals to conduct operations and achieve reasonable military goals.

Hamdani: I totally agree with you, but there was also real leadership within the Iraqi army. First-rate leaders rose up, while the political leadership had no choice but to go back to real military capabilities. A perfect example is Abd al-Hakim Amer who as a major was promoted to commander of the whole Egyptian army, because of his competence, which underlies the disconnect with times before the conflict.[27] And General Sa'd al-Din el-Shathili, who had a totally different vision than Gamal Abdal-Nassir. He was a more realistic professional, rather than a politician.[28] He was not influenced by parties during any conflict. The young professional officers within the Iraqi army continued to work until the Ba'athist political party came to power. The Ba'athists actually raised [the level of the army] and accelerated many promotions for young officers before the conflict with Iran.

Woods: Specific examples of who emerged from 1973 as the professional generals, and the professional leaders, would be helpful. But tell us about what happened in that period when the Ba'ath party, or at least Saddam's version of it, took firm control in 1979, just before the war. Was there a distinct change in the professional soldiers and leaders in that period before the Iran-Iraq War? How did the intellectual heroes and real leaders of 1973 fare just before the war with Iran?

Hamdani: The Ba'ath party was in power in 1968 in Iraq, but it influenced the military leadership because of the confrontations with Israel, and this presented a dilemma. The party wanted to push the careers of the loyal young military officers, but, at the same time, for the most part it did not sacrifice the level of military professionalism during the time of crisis. Our slogan at the time was, "Better a good soldier than a good Ba'athist!" The turning point came when Saddam Hussein arrived in total control in mid-1979. He quickly gained the reputation of promoting young leaders who were loyal Ba'athists instead of real professional soldiers.

So for the first time in the history of the Iraqi army, there were a large number of promotions for political reasons. At that time, in 1979, I was still at the staff college. I watched as Saddam promoted Lieutenant Colonel Hisham to brigadier general, as well as to command one of the first-line divisions. Another officer, Lieutenant Colonel Khaled . . . was also promoted to brigadier general, and became commander of the 3ᵈ Division, our best. Another was a staff major, Tali Ad-Duri, who was made a full colonel and commander of the 9ᵗʰ Division. Another was Mahmoud Shukr Shahin, promoted from colonel to brigadier general and who then became commander of the 6ᵗʰ Division. So these first four promotions were a major shock for the Iraqi army. All were very dramatic promotions. Then the war with Iran began.

Murray: Did this have a large impact on the professionalization of the Iraqi army, now that political loyalty became more important than professional competence?

Hamdani: This is correct. By the time we got to the war with Iran, the basic culture of the army had changed because of Saddam's actions. He ordered politicians to serve at the army level and promoted himself to the military rank [of marshal]. He also emphasized the principle, a very dangerous saying, that as long as one was a Ba'athist he can always be a leader, since the Ba'athist is a truly natural leader. Therefore, there was no problem in a Ba'athist switching from being a politician to a military leader.

Woods: Given all that you have explained about the Iraqi army learning after 1967 and 1973, and what you described as the professionalizing processes in your first couple of years as a relatively junior officer—by then you were a staff major, becoming a lieutenant colonel—do you remember talking to your peers? Did professional soldiers like yourself really know and dread the implications of this process of politicization? Did you regard this step as a giant step backward from where you had been in the years leading up to the conflict?

Hamdani: This became a complex within the Iraqi military ranks because we knew as professional military officers that we would pay hard and dearly for Saddam's actions in politicizing the army. Nevertheless, most of us knew that our duty was to continue to try to be a better military professional and not to try and get involved in political processes. Unfortunately, because of Saddam's dictatorship, we had to keep silent.

There was even a good and respectful man, by the name of Adnan Khairallah, whom Saddam promoted from colonel to the deputy general commander of the armed forces (or the minister of defense). Even this good man, whom we deeply respected and who had the right attitude, we did not feel that he was yet qualified for the position, but rather had received the position because Saddam Hussein had married Khairallah's sister, and so they were brothers-in-law.

Discussion Two

Iraqi Military and Political Transition through the 1970s—Prologue to Iran-Iraq War—Transition of Iranian Leadership and Military—The Decision to Invade—Saddam's Aspirations—Earliest Phase of the War—Political and Professional Soldiers—Disorganized Command and Control of Iranian Operations

Holaday: During the transitions after 1967 and 1973, the Iraqi military apparently learned many lessons and further professionalized its officer corps. However, during this time, a parallel process—the introduction of Ba'ath-loyal military officers to the higher ranks—seemed to contradict this [learning] progress. The military officers focused on threats from Israel and Iran while the political leadership seemed more concerned with internal dissent and the security of the regime itself. Did this split describe a larger tension between the domestically focused Ba'athist political leadership and the professional military-focused and regional orientation of the officers, one that continued through the subsequent decades?

Hamdani: Well, as a matter of fact, there was not a complete change of military leadership as of 1979. The Ba'athist officers reached division leadership positions. There were professionals at a higher level than divisions. . . . we [professional soldiers] were among those professionals. We used to query them to reach out to the highest expertise available. We had more respect for the corps commanders because we considered them the real professional soldiers and commanders—many had been our instructors when we were at the [military] academy and staff college.

This [tension] had a considerable impact during the course of the Iran-Iraq conflict. The first shock came at the onset of the war with Iran, when I was a staff major and commander of an armored reconnaissance battalion. At the time, I felt that a strategic mistake had been made. But, actually, neither of the two sides, Iraqi or Iranian, had a real understanding of the nature of the conflict we were entering.

You see, each war has its own nature. The war with Israel [1973] had its own nature, and this was different from the nature of the war of the Kurdish insurgency [1974–1975], or the war with Iran [1980–1988], or the war with the Kurdish alliance [post-1991], and different from the nature of this last war in 2003. We experienced this reality directly; we felt and lived it on the ground, where we had only read about it before. When you move from one war to another, you realize there are major differences in character between each conflict. This was the difference between the political and professional members of the military—they had different perspectives about the nature of the war upon which they were about to embark.

Woods: I'd like you to put yourself back into 1978–1979, the period when Iraq's focus was on the Israeli military, focusing westward, as you described. The situation included the collapse of the Shah, starting in 1978, and then the emergence of the Iranian revolution in 1979, and finally a new regime in Iran. Thus, a revolutionary regime arose that was obviously of great concern to the Ba'ath party. Iraq now had a strategic challenge to the east. What do you remember about your understanding of the new political threats in the east? This seems to have been a dramatic change from 13 years of focusing on the military challenge to the west. What level of understanding did you have as a soldier about the potential adversary in Iran?

Hamdani: When this change started, and Khomeini emerged in Iran, we did not have any other understanding about the regime and its capabilities, other than what we knew about the Shah's army. I mean, we had no idea what was happening to the Iranian army. All we knew was that the Iranian military had significant capabilities, along with a first-rate American armament—for instance, the F–14 aircraft was something big, a truly advanced aircraft. They also had trained division staffs in many places, units that used to go from Iran to the United States for training. Therefore, we looked at the Iranian army as similar to the Israeli army, but maybe half as effective.

We hated the Shah's government, because the Shah interfered with the Kurds and other Iraqi causes internally. He had interests in the Shatt al-Arab and the Gulf area. He imposed himself as the police officer of the Arab Gulf. But after 1975, he became an echo of history for us.[29] There weren't any real problems with Iran, at least until the religious scholars mobilized their large and zealous population—then this became a scary thing for the surrounding countries and the region.

We heard of the revolutionary changes inside Iran that largely wrecked the Iranian army. That is, the Iranian army collapsed with the Shah's regime, and a popular revolutionary army started to emerge as its replacement. This appeared as a dark cloud. How could this strong, well-equipped, well-trained army just fall away with the regime to be replaced by just farmers and religious folk? We could not believe that the Shah's army, with its American style and support, was not actually able to protect the Shah's government. We had many worries over this transformation, wondering about the impact of these new religious leaders and scholars within the new Iranian army, and its possible impact on the Iraqi army, for example—especially the beliefs of the new leaders, who would bring the Middle East back to the stone age with their street education. So in brief, the Shah's army, built over long years, collapsed like an avalanche. Nobody expected this.

Now when we looked toward Iran, there were Islamic militias made up of farmers, workers, small groups, and [even] soldiers from the Shah's army. This is when Saddam Hussein began to think about laying out a plan to destroy this army, because it was not nearly as strong as the Shah's army had been. He saw this as the perfect moment, which Iraq needed to seize, because the Iranians were not well equipped, trained, or capable of fighting, and so he could eliminate the Iranian threat.

In Iraq, the atmosphere emphasized the political and religious threats against the Ba'athist state, all in a frantic media. The Iranian religious scholars tried to export the revolution across the border. So the Iraqi government was under wide pressure from the Shia in Iraq, who were rallying and trying to manipulate the situation to benefit from the revolution in Iran or maybe even to implement the same thing in Iraq.

Woods: At that point in time, the Arab Shia and Iraqi Shia made up a large percentage of the regular army in Iraq, right? Did you have concerns about the revolutionary influence within the Iraqi military as a junior officer? Was this Iranian influence a concern, and was it something you had to work against as an officer? In other words, was preventing revolutionary agitation within your forces a real concern for the average unit and junior officer?

Hamdani: As a matter of fact, we did not think about the Shia or Sunni percentage issue then. The [Ba'athist] Iraqi state was not built on divisions, but on respect, and on technocrats. We knew that the percentage of Shia was high and that their numbers were large, not only in the army, but in all state institutions. The problem was that the Da'wa party adopted the same goal as the Iranian revolution and acted as a supporting hand for Iran in Iraq.[30] They had both political as well as military members working for their long-term agenda in Iraq, and soon became active with the support of Khomeini's government.

Murray: It seems that in 1980, both Khomeini's and Saddam's regimes sought war as a means to ease internal difficulties, but also because of a bizarre underestimation of the will and the long-term capabilities of their opponents.

Hamdani: This is true, but to be precise, Iraq had no hostile intentions. It started receiving direct threats from Iran, and this is what made Saddam think of a preventative and useful war. Truly, Iran was the one who launched its threats from inside Iraq through the Da'wa party. It was a strange situation. We had young [Shia] officers within the military and the air force, trying to sabotage aircraft and destroy tanks and acting on behalf of the revolution in Iran. The Iranian clerics believed that Saddam was atheist because his regime was secular. They were represented by the group of . . . Ibrahim Al-Ja'afari.[31]

We, like other soldiers in the world, believed that our weapon was our honor. A soldier is not allowed to put his gun down. So the [sabotage] operations to disrupt aircraft, weapons, and armor all began under the guidance of Iran. This scared us, because it represented a change in loyalty from the military service and the goals and honor of the army. How could someone destroy his own weapons; for whom would he do this?

Woods: Let's explore the Iraqi objectives in the very early stages of the military conflict. What kind of military objectives could stop the Shia revolutionary intent inside Iraq? As described, these were long-term activities, with the Da'wa party seeking long-term influence. How was the military instrument supposed to reach out and stop that process from your perspective? For example, was the intent to intimidate the Iranian government, or just to destabilize the revolution and force the Iranians to look internally and stop looking at Iraq? What were Iraqi military operations supposed to accomplish in terms of the larger problem of Iranian influence?

Figure 3. **The initial Iraqi invasion of Iran, September 1980**

Source: Satellite image courtesy of National Aeronautics and Space Administration. Available at <www.parstimes.com/spaceimages/mideast/>.

Hamdani: The decision to go to war with Iran rested on several assumptions. The first was to prevent the exportation of the Iranian revolution to Iraq. The second was that the new Iranian army at the time was still in the early stages of formation, while the Shah's army was dissolving. This presented an opportunity to attack when [the Iranians] were weak. The Iraqi leadership figured that if the Iraqi armies advanced approximately 10–20 kilometers deep into Iran along the borders, Khomeini would have to send [Iranian] forces from the surrounding area of Tehran to the borders. This would leave Tehran exposed, and give the opportunity to the Mehdi Bazargan group to revolt against the religious leadership and gain control of Tehran.[32] So the idea was to bring the militia out of Tehran to weaken the revolution for a counterrevolution [see figure 3].

Murray: There is a wonderful quote in your memoir, where you say, "Both political systems lacked strategic vision; they fell easily into the great trap set for them by the major Western powers." I would argue that there was no trap set, because, in fact, the West did not have any policy, either.

Hamdani: There are a few points I'd like to make so that we can better understand how to evaluate the war, if you'd allow me to go into them. We see that both militaries were a part of Third World countries, and, on both sides, the regimes filled up their military institutions in the higher positions according to political loyalty rather than expertise. Additionally, both political leaderships failed to allow the professional military officers to participate in making military decisions. Rather, decisions occurred with political intent down to the lowest level—all the way down to the company level. Both militaries lacked senior level officers sufficiently competent to understand the concept of long-term strategy. But even if these capabilities had existed, or if there were a handful of officers who did have the understanding, their influence was disrupted by the political regimes at all levels. The political limits had a paralyzing effect on virtually every decision. Furthermore, both armies suffered from a limited level of education for both soldiers and officers. Regarding armaments, both armies relied on importing weaponry and other equipment.

Murray: The situation was analogous to World War I in 1914, where nobody understood either the strategy or the political framework of the war. Everybody expected the war to be short and then, in fact, everybody had to adapt under the worst kind of circumstances—mainly huge casualties and suffering on both sides.

Hamdani: No one has ever planned for a long war—this is a situation that humankind has repeated throughout time. Everyone thinks a certain action will happen and refuses to expect the war to be long. Just as in World War I, World War II, or any war, the Iraqi leadership did not expect the war with Iran to last for more than 8 weeks.

Politicians always base their plans on winning the war, and they impose this plan on military leaders. This puts more pressure on the military to execute, even if they lack the capability to do so. [Georges] Clemenceau, the French prime minister, said, "War is so important that one should not leave it to just the generals." Then, during World War II, General [Charles] De Gaulle commented, "War is too important to leave it to the politicians alone." The truth is they were both right, but only if we combine the two aphorisms.

This is the problem—there are no clear limits between politics and war. Determining this requires cleverness and talent. Where are the limits of politics and where are the limits of war? Figuring out this balance is where genius, talent, and experience show.

The war, or the disaster that happened to Iraq, in my personal analysis, is the same problem that confronted the American administration in 2003—the interference of politicians in war, more than should have been the case. The actions of former Defense Secretary Donald Rumsfeld and Paul Wolfowitz, both of whom were politicians, to influence and pressure commanders on the ground did not give the officers the freedom to operate from their knowledge and expertise. Of course, General Tommy Franks did not argue or resist their influence on the military—and this is what affected the current crisis in Iraq so disastrously.

General Colin Powell, as Secretary of State, was speaking from a clearer perspective on the military affairs than was the Pentagon. While Colin Powell was involved in foreign affairs, he was thinking more realistically from a military perspective than were the folks in the Pentagon. So as Dr. Murray noted, the problem of leaders not understanding the character of the war in which they are engaged . . . this will continue to remain problematic, whether in First World or Third World countries.

Woods: The problems and the challenges that we are discussing today are probably much more universal than we often like to admit.

Going back to 1980, I would like to ask about some specific events, such as some you covered in your memoir. Can you describe for me the period between 4 and 22 September 1980? You discussed what you called the series of quick raids by the 6th Armored Division and the 1st Mechanized Division, around 18 September—just before the main invasion. Can you explain the operational issues before the invasion on 22 September? What kind of operations were these? Were they part of the preparation for the main invasion, or just part of a preemptive strategy? How much of this activity was designed to draw the militias out of Tehran and to intimidate the regime, and so forth?

Hamdani: As a matter of fact, it was a preparatory and necessary stage prior to the war, because of Iranian shelling of villages along the Iraqi side of the border. Those villages were supposed to become mobilization areas, safe for [Iraqi] troops—so this required pushing the Iranian artillery back so that the mobilization areas were safe, prior to the arrival of the main force.

Woods: So these operations were designed to secure what [the United States] calls the "line of departure." These operations were designed to secure the border area in preparation for the actual movement across the Shatt al-Arab.

Hamdani: The [Ba'ath] party leadership met with the State Command in Abu Ghraib, on 6 July 1980, and made the decision to launch the war against Iran.[33] Then on 7 July, the military and military leaders were informed of the decision to go to war. However, they were not told when the war was to begin. Instead, they were just ordered to begin preparations for the war. So there was no exact day [given] as to when it was going to take place. On 4 September, the early stage operations to secure the mobilization areas started.

Murray: Could you put yourself in the Iranians' shoes? Why were they doing harassing fire along the border? Did they feel that war was inevitable, or were they trying to push Iraq into military operations? What do you think their long-term military and political goals in terms of these actions were?

Hamdani: I believe that their first purpose was to confirm the presence of the Iranian force. To say to Iraq that their army had not collapsed yet, that it was still a strong army, and could still influence things. The Iranian army was calling out to its adversary that it still stood strong. The second objective was to send a message to the Da'wa party, which was politically active and had carried out a number of acts of sabotage and terrorism over the summer of 1980, that there is a strong force that would support it.[34] The Iranian leadership was confident that the Iraqi regime was ripe to collapse from any internal or external shock. These Iranian actions [aimed at] expediting the overthrow of [Saddam's Ba'ath] regime.

We had to understand that the Islamic Revolutionary Guard had started to dominate in Iran, but that the units carrying out orders were not a part of a centralized, comprehensive plan. Their actions started from different power centers with different agendas. This probably played a role. We're seeing similar things in Iraq today, where there are various forces following different political agendas, based on different [Islamic] scholars.

Woods: General Hamdani, you describe in your memoirs some specific events surrounding the Iraqi 12th Armored Division, as well as the 4th and 8th Divisions. You wrote how in the early weeks of the fighting [September-October 1980], there was considerable confusion on the operational command level, and on the staff planning level. You wrote that logistics and operational orders were unclear. In fact, you noted that the division commanders were not even clear on what their final objectives were. Were these events the result of the new class of generals? Or was this operation of such a scale that the Iraqi military had not adequately prepared for large-scale multicorps operations?

Hamdani: The problem was bad planning. There was no accurate or specific planning. The operation did not rest on the facts of a position. This was a result of weak leaders, who simply wanted to speed up the process. They even stopped the gathering of intelligence.

Murray: Was Saddam, in particular, pushing the planning forward?

Hamdani: The political decision was rushed. The plan for war needed more time and more preparations. It had been too little, and the intelligence on which it rested was weak.

Murray: It seems that Saddam's picture of the world in the summer of 1980 was that Iraq was in a position to assume the role that Egypt had played, as the leader of the Arab world. In particular, Saddam seems to have viewed the Iranian confrontation as a way to quickly put himself in a position as the great leader, who could then lead [the Arabs] in the great effort against Israel.

Hamdani: This is absolutely true. As a matter of fact, this does not only apply to Saddam Hussein, but to any leader with great ambition. Political leaders will not be memorialized, except through war. Political leaders will take advantage of a war for their interests. When Saddam Hussein entered the scene, like any ambitious political leader, he knew that no political leader would be memorialized in history, except with victory in war.

Woods: General Hamdani, as you have described operations in the Iraqi II Corps in October of 1980, I was struck by the reaction of the corps commander to your inspection reports from the divisions on the lack of patrolling and intelligence. You quote the corps commanders as saying, "You're [Hamdani] ruining our morale, stop complaining about the reality of the battlefield. . . . you're ruining the morale of the force!" Can you describe this particular commander for me? Was he one of the political generals you were discussing earlier? What was your reaction to his statement? How did his subordinates react?

Hamdani: The problem was that most of the division commanders at the time were not competent commanders. We [the professional soldiers] looked at things differently because [the political generals] came into those commanding positions due to their loyalty to the [Ba'ath] party.

At the time, I was in command of a reconnaissance battalion, and I had a number of specific tasks. My division commander was one of the worst division commanders, since he was one of these [Ba'ath] appointees. He did not fully understand his role and how to protect his sector, in this case regarding the sector for our paratroopers' airdrop. Because of his incompetence, I had to carry out his [responsibilities] in addition to all of my tasks.

Murray: It strikes me that this sudden politicization of the Iraqi army, which occurred in the space of the 2 years before the war, was driven by Saddam's fears. This created a situation, which if we look at it in terms of the military history of the 20th century, we see that effective military organizations are those where the reports become more and more critical the higher up the ranks one moves. On the other hand, in ineffective military organizations, the reports become rosier and more optimistic the higher the command level. In other words, effective military organizations not only demand bad as well as good news, but are more critical of their subordinates, whereas the Iraqi army suffered from this suppression of bad news.

Hamdani: This is the difference between the political objectives and the military objectives. We had to learn about the field beforehand. If it were bad, we would know it was bad. But a politician would tell you that it is fine.

Murray: General, you described an incident from 9 October 1980, when you captured an Iranian lieutenant. You wrote how this Iranian POW [prisoner of war] described the internal conflicts between the Iranian regular army and the revolutionary guards. It strikes me that, whereas the Iraqi military was a top-down structured, politically dominated military in 1980, that the Iranian problem was that it was not just a conflict among different power centers, but in fact all sorts of independent centers trying to manipulate the course of events in this revolutionary situation. In fact, it could be that the artillery fire in September before the war began could really have been some mullah at the front line saying, "Fire at them!" In other words, local leaders deliberately trying to start a war. As you have described it, the Iranian situation was so "revolutionary and chaotic" that nobody was running the show.

Hamdani: This is definitely possible. At the time, there was no pyramidal structure or decisionmaking process within the Iranian army. It only had Khomeini at the top, and everyone was vying to prove [himself] to Khomeini or to get closer to the leader by showing his role in fighting the Iraqis. There was a conflict between all the people underneath Khomeini over who could satisfy him. And the way to do this was to retaliate against the Iraqi forces on the borders. So there was no coordination. They operated with their own political agendas as ways of getting closer to Khomeini.

Discussion Three

Early Use of Airpower — SIGINT [Signals Intelligence] — Winter 1980 – 1981 Iraqi Command Changes — Saddam's Response to Failure and Executions — 1980–1982 Losses and Army Expansions — Developments of Iranian and Iraqi Forces

Woods: Let's move on to a few doctrinal topics. Could you describe your impression of how both the Iraqi and Iranian military used airpower in the early years of the war? What was your overall impression of the Iranians' use of airpower?

Hamdani: For starters, both the Iraqi and Iranian armies suffered from shortages in their air forces and air defenses. In neither area were they complete at first. They lacked the technologies, the expertise, and the funding to provide for and develop their air capabilities. But we took the Iranian air forces as a competent force that could surpass the Iraqi air force, especially as it had the technological support from the United States. However, there was a balance to that, because they had internal political issues and loyalty problems due to the revolution. A large number of their air force pilots were not able to participate in exercises because the regime believed them to be disloyal to the Islamic government, and so they were not allowed to participate in the conflict between Iran and Iraq. So just because the Iranians had superior capabilities and better equipment, that did not mean they were able to use them.

In the beginning, the Iraqi air force tried to carry out an air attack on Iranian air force bases, similar to the Israeli air attack on the Egyptians in 1967. Unfortunately, this strike did not achieve its goals, because the Iraqi air force at the time was in a transitional period and had not yet moved forward. In order for the strike to succeed, we required air capabilities to carry out long-range missions, but we lacked that capability. It is true we had the Tu-22 [supersonic bomber and reconnaissance aircraft] and it was able to go deep enough to bomb Tehran, but the range of the protecting fighter aircraft was insufficient, and we could not perform air refueling.[35] The other problem was that the Iraqi air force did not have the ability to jam the radars in the depth of Iran, so the Iranians quickly identified our aircraft at a considerable distance. As a result, our bomber pilots flew at low altitudes between valleys, so that the enemy would not detect them by radar. They succeeded in the early phases in their first attempts, but then the Iranians learned the flight patterns and were able to stop our attacks.

Iran gave orders through the Da'wa party to soldiers affiliated with the party who were working in aircraft maintenance to sabotage six of the bombers inside Iraqi bases. The Iraqi air force also lacked missiles that had night guidance systems, and so its aircraft had limited accuracy, thus requiring a larger number of bombs to achieve its objectives.

Woods: You are describing what we call interdiction missions or deep fight. On the other side of the airpower coin, along the front, when you were a reconnaissance commander, did you employ fixed-wing or helicopters in the close fight? Was that something that you had much experience with in 1980, and were there any examples of such an employment of close air support?

Hamdani: The Iranians were more capable than we were in using helicopters. For us they represented an advanced weapons system. The majority of helicopters available [to the Iranians] were American Cobras, provided by the United States to the Shah, and they were good. On the Iraqi side, we used either the French Gazelle [helicopter] or the Soviet MiG–25 [FOXBAT ground attack aircraft]. As the war progressed, there was a change in the capabilities, as Iraqi air capabilities steadily increased, while Iranian capabilities decreased due to the lack of maintenance, support, and imported spare parts.

The first time the Iraqi air force planned and fully utilized its helicopters was on 27 October 1980. The planning and usage of 100 percent of the Iraqi army's aviation capabilities produced good results. However, there was a problem in that both sides exaggerated the losses their aircraft caused to the enemy. The exaggeration was abnormal. Another problem was the Iraqi air force's lack of knowledge in and about their own aircraft. They could not differentiate during battle between Iraqi aircraft and Iranian aircraft. This caused a considerable number of incidents of friendly fire, especially when ground forces were using the SA–7 [shoulder-fired surface-to-air missile]. We lost many Iraqi aircraft as a result. This led Iraqi commanders to shut down the entire air defense system during any campaign where our helicopters or aircraft were in play in order to avoid friendly fire losses. At the same time, this meant that Iranian helicopters would show up, and there would be no response from the air defenses.

I remember an incident in the middle of one battle, when I was on top of a hill and saw two Iranian Cobras [attack helicopters] coming from behind our forces and firing at ground targets. They were flying so low that I could actually see the pilot and his long beard. I gave orders for the ground forces to respond, but they replied they had orders to do nothing, because everything was shut down, so that they could not use their antiair capabilities.

During the early stages of the war, the air forces of the opposing sides had only a secondary role in the conflict, especially on the frontline fighting and close to the border. Over the course of the conflict, their role developed. The ability to distinguish aircraft on the part of air defense operators improved, and we noticed this change. The problem that emerged later was that the Iranians sealed the gaps that the Iraqi aircraft had exploited early in the conflict, as they improved.

Murray: Were there any indications that the Iranians were intercepting Iraqi radio transmissions, or using any kind of signals intelligence? Did they show any initial capability to collect signals intelligence, or did Iran develop that capability during the course of the war?

Hamdani: Well, they relied on regular equipment for their superiority, because the Iraqi side had more and better electronic warfare (EW) equipment. The Iranians also had EW equipment, but it was limited, so they relied mostly on spies. We could identify their troop movements by using ground radar systems, such as the Rasit.[36] In the reconnaissance battalion I commanded, we were able to detect small animals with our radar and could read every kind of sound pattern. The men of the radar reconnaissance platoon started to know the difference between a tank engine, a car engine, and other engines related to the area. But one day, one of the soldiers said, "I don't know what this is." From the sound, it was indeed strange. Therefore, I sent a combat patrol to this place. In fact, it was a donkey moving around in a bizarre way, since its legs were tied up.

The electronic warfare equipment was largely a French program that we had and started in 1976, so this gave us an advantage over the Iranians, on the tactical as well as the strategic level.[37] We gained useful information, such as when and where the Iranian troops were going to move, with great accuracy.

Woods: In your memoir, you mentioned that in late November [1980] there were changes of command in the Iraqi military. Specifically, you noted that Saddam relieved the II Corps commander in January 1981. Were these changes of Iraqi military leadership in late 1980 and early 1981 a direct result of poor performance of those division and corps commanders? Was this a signal that Saddam realized that perhaps his political generals were not performing as he had hoped?

Hamdani: The first reason for their removal was that the Iraqi forces were expanding horizontally. We had begun the war with only 37 brigades. When we first engaged on 22 September, the 37 brigades had the task of performing their operations in great geographic depth and breadth, but the war did not end there— the Iranian counteroffensives began. So there were many gaps and there was a need to expand the Iraqi army, and a corresponding need to reorganize the leadership, expand it, and promote a number of officers.

Some commanders failed, while others succeeded, regardless of the reason for the failure. This pushed Saddam to promote those who succeeded and eliminate those in leadership positions who had failed, providing more opportunity for the younger officers.

The problem with Saddam was that he understood excellence in command as only a matter of courage. Therefore, he concentrated on courageous people, even if they were stupid and for the most part disregarded expertise and professionalism.

Woods: There is much mythology and rumor about the way Saddam dealt with failures on the battlefield, especially in the early years of the Iran-Iraq War. The stories say that if commanders did not perform or did not show proper courage, he had them executed. It seems difficult to know whether this occurred. Do you have any knowledge or personal experience of commanders whom Saddam pulled off the battlefield, stripped of command, and then actually executed for poor performance?

Hamdani: This is a tough topic for those officers who, when [Saddam] started [promoting political generals], knew that the war was going to take longer and be harder than Saddam conceived. It became clear that our capabilities were not sufficient once the Iranians started to strike us with continuous counterattacks. Saddam put great pressure on Iraqi commanders on the ground to avoid losses, which led them not to report failures.[38] Withholding losses from reports and thus not receiving reinforcements or other support left commanders in impossible combat conditions. However, this was better than reporting their failures and suffering execution. The executions started with high-ranking officers and then worked their way down through the ranks.

Woods: Can you remember the most prominent examples of [battlefield executions] from the first year of the war?

Hamdani: The first one executed was the commander of the 2^d Brigade in the Beit Sa'ad region, Staff Lieutenant Colonel Muhammad Juwad Kadhum, at the beginning of 1981. After that, Saddam had a company commander and soldiers of the same brigade executed. In 1982, the III Corps commander, Major General Salah Al-Qadi, was executed. Then Brigadier General Juwad Asaad, the commander of the 3^d Division, followed.

Murray: In the 1980–1982 timeframe, both the Iraqi army and the Iranian army engaged in ferocious combat with major ongoing military operations and heavy losses among both NCOs [noncommissioned officers] as well as officers. At the same time, the structures of both armies were expanding rapidly. Can you explain how effectively this was done, what sorts of choices were made, what worked, what did not work, and who did a better job expanding their military forces—the Iranians or the Iraqis?

Hamdani: Well, first of all, both parties did not expect a long war. There was strategic advice to the Ba'ath party claiming that if Iraq forces were to advance a distance of 10–20 kilometers into Iranian territory, the political situation would change in Tehran with Khomeini's overthrow. On the other hand, the Iranians believed that if their army advanced toward the Iraqi border, Baghdad would fall, since there would be an Islamic revolution among the Shia. So both parties did not expect the war to be long, and this forced them both to mobilize their nations.

With regard to expansion, Iraq had less trouble because the Iranian military was undergoing a fundamental change from being the military established by the Shah to reorganizing itself as a religious army. Iraq kept the same structure and just had to increase recruitment. We did not worry as much as the Iranians about restructuring hierarchies.

The Iranian army relied on the Pasdaran force, which was the Islamic Revolutionary Guards—it started to expand that force at the expense of the traditional Iranian army. The other organization that emerged was the Basij, or the volunteers. Its units consisted of poor rural folk, who volunteered to fight, but who received little or no training and only light weapons.

The Iraqi military, on the other hand, was expanding and increasing its armaments, its air force, artillery, armor, and so forth. Therefore, it already improved in terms of technology and the nature of the troops. The Iranian military formed a new kind of religious army that believed in a religious doctrine. So the Iranians had three different forces: the traditional army, which steadily weakened, with the air force attached to it; the Pasdaran, or Islamic Revolutionary Guards, which expanded to become the main force and which gained air and naval forces; and the Basij volunteers, whom the Iranians gathered from villages with religious rhetoric. The last only got speeches without training. We called them "livestock herds." The Iranians used the Basij for one-time missions on the front.

Both sides had advantages, though. The Iranians clearly had a major geographic advantage, where they felt comfortable with the defensive depth of their country, since no Iraqi attacks could reach deep enough to disrupt Khomeini's regime (by ground or air). For us, we could never relax, because we had little strategic depth. A simple comparison of the distances of the two capital cities from the border underlines this point. Iranian soldiers were approximately 116 kilometers from Baghdad, while Iraqi soldiers were 800 kilometers from Tehran. Tehran always possessed a comfortable buffer zone.

Moreover, Iranian forces were three times larger than Iraqi forces; they had a larger human population than we did. Their mobilization system rested on a war season. On normal days, they would have no problem with frontline support, whereas we would have to maintain full capabilities throughout the year, since we were in a defensive strategic situation.

The spiritual, moral, and religious influence of Ayatollah Khomeini was strong at the beginning of the revolution, and so this had a tremendous psychological impact on the Iranian people. Their soldiers were willing to do anything, such as walking through minefields and suffering huge losses. They believed that Karbala was crucial and was just across the border, so that they had to do whatever it took to execute the mission.

Our technical side started to improve steadily, while it weakened on the Iranian side. So the mobilization system of Iraq was better than that of Iran, since it could exploit about 60 percent of the country's manpower, while the Iranian side used only 20 percent. But this also represented a weakness, for this meant using 60 percent of the total manpower during the war. Regardless of the increases in Iraqi expertise, the Iranians possessed an overwhelming number of forces.

Woods: Can you expand on the purpose of the Pasdaran and the Iranian popular forces a little more?

Hamdani: The purpose of building up the popular Iranian forces was to compensate for the threat they believed the secular Iraqi army posed. The victories of the Iraqi army over the faithful of Iran struck a nerve in Khomeini's ideology, since he believed it was impossible for the faithful to lose. He had wanted to gain the support of the Iraqi Shia, but this did not happen, and so this may have affected his long-term planning.

Woods: Paralleling the growth of the Iranian Pasdaran and Basij was the growth in the Iraqi popular army. Could you tell us about what the Iraqi popular army provided the regime and the overall war effort that Iraq was not getting from the regular army? Was it a way to hurry up and push bodies to the front, and thus skip or minimize the training, or were there other purposes for the popular army?

Hamdani: Iraq needed to mobilize the largest possible number of Iraqi people and weapons. Later on there was a greater emphasis on vertical expansion and competence, but at this point there was a horizontal increase, which decreased the level of competence in the Iraqi armed forces. That decreased to the point where the army could no longer expand horizontally. So there was a need for troops in depth, for defense, maintenance, and depots, and this created the push to form the popular army. The popular army worked for 2 or 3 months at a time, because 60 percent of the workforce was unavailable for the normal economy. Therefore, Saddam created a system where this popular army would fulfill defense duties for 2 or 3 months only, and then return to the civilian sector, so that there would be a balance between the normal economy's workforce and the manpower required for the war effort.

Discussion Four

Saddam's Psychology and Personality Development — January 1981 Armor Battle — Iranian Human Wave Tactics and Iraqi Minefields — Khomeini's Spiritual Influence — Battles of Abadan and Khorramshahr — Loss of Special Forces — End of Initial Iraqi Offensives in May 1981

Murray: Let us turn to Saddam Hussein for a little while. It seems that during the course of the Iran-Iraq War, he began to recognize that military professionalism was something he needed, and yet it also appears that his instincts and desires were, as soon as the Iran-Iraq War was over, to get rid of it and return to the system he was developing before the war. This seems to be a pattern that runs through his entire reign—going back and forth—but always having the instinct for a need for political reliability, rather than professional competence.

Hamdani: This is true. There is no doubt that Saddam Hussein was smart enough where, at the beginning of the war, he relied on the military expertise as much as possible—especially those at the Ministry of Defense and the general staff of the army. For example, Saddam relied on General Abd al-Jabbar Shanshal to a considerable extent, a man who was professional and had experience, but at the same time loyal and not hostile to Saddam. There were also some assistants—such as General Abd al-Jabbar al-Asadi, and others who were not Ba'athists, but professionals.[39] The division commanders were loyal to Saddam, as most were Ba'athists. At the same time, Saddam was betting his future success on this war. If he did not succeed, his legacy would be affected. So he had to rely on military expertise. He gave his generals authority and respect, but this was not necessarily out of an understanding of the nature of war, since he was not a military man. He thought that he could learn through those people during the war by placing himself in the battlefield.

Saddam Hussein said about himself in a meeting with intellectuals of the Arab Organization at the beginning of the war, "I engaged in war and I don't have information at a higher level than captain in the Iraqi army, while I am the general leader of the armed forces." He was honest when he mentioned this, but while confessing this ignorance of the country's military opponents, he was also trying to display how commanders, including himself, learn and gain experience and expertise through the war. Saddam felt that he could back down on everything, give away positions and power, but he could not afford to lose the war against Iran.

Woods: Modern armor battles are rare enough that I was struck by a description of one that you wrote about in your memoirs that occurred during January 1981 between the Iraqi 10th Armored [Brigade] and the Iranian 16th Armored [Division]. Could you describe the character of the battle, how big it was, the sorts of maneuvers involved, and what precipitated it?

Hamdani: Well, the Iraqi 10th Armored Brigade carried out a counterattack on the Iranian 16th Armored Division and inflicted major damages on it. Our armored battalions were certainly much better than the Iranian armored because our armored units had fought in the October War and trained in light of the lessons learned from the wars with the Israeli forces in 1967 and 1973.

The Iraqi armor was also superior just on pure technology. The Russian T–72 tank was better than the British Challenger. Moreover, the T–72's maneuverability was superior since it is lighter and is more flexible.

Murray: Getting back to Saddam—from your perspective, what were Saddam's strengths and weaknesses, when looking at the man as a whole, not just specifically from a military or political perspective, but in terms of watching him over the long period that you did? How would you sum him up generally?

Hamdani: Well, Saddam Hussein is a most complex personality. We might even say that he possessed several personalities. We can analyze Saddam Hussein's personality according to the theories of [Sigmund] Freud or [Alfred] Adler, or even [Ivan] Pavlov. We need the theories of these psychologists in order to analyze Saddam's personality. And this is not an easy thing; his personality was very complex. I mention these three psychologists because they bring in different elements: Freud was the founder of the theory of the analytical method in psychology; Adler is the one who developed what we call the "inferiority complex," while Pavlov talked about the adaptability of character—the capacity for adaptation. So we need these three to explain Saddam's personality and provide insights into its complexity. The inferiority complex suggests that people behave the way they do because of a lack of confidence in certain areas. Pavlov's discussion of the adaptability of character explains that an individual's personal character or behavior is something he or she assumes or copies from others to cover up other weaknesses. Saddam had a very strong, powerful, and charismatic personality.

Woods: What historical character would you say he is closest to?

Hamdani: He had a combination of Hitler's and Stalin's personalities. He was strong and firm, like iron, as Stalin was, and courageous. He had a unique, unreal courage. He was also like Hitler, in his inferiority complex. By playing the persona of a great general and putting himself in the position as the commander in chief of Iraq's armed forces, he hoped to cover over the gaps of his military knowledge and thus compensate for his shortcoming. Saddam's personality embraced most virtues as well as most vices. As a reader and listener, he was precise and careful. At other times, he would totally shut off others from participating in the dialogue, and conversation would become totally one-way. Saddam possessed a personality that at one moment might kill the closest person to him, a member of his family, without a care; then the next moment he would be extremely sensitive, tears in his eyes over the injury of a cat. He had this kind of double personality.

Holaday: Was he aware of these behavioral and mood changes in himself? Did he recognize some of these things about himself?

Hamdani: We cannot call it schizophrenia, but Saddam lived a life of impersonation, where every personality would emerge in an instant. For instance, in one moment, you would find Saddam Hussein the intellectual, who would think as deeply as a philosopher would over a subject, as a good leader or decisionmaker. The next moment he would be like a naïve and backward farmer. He would switch from being a civilized person to the stubborn Bedouin personality he held deep within himself. This switching back and forth is what people who dealt with him could not stand.

As he got older, his violence and impulsiveness decreased, but his state of isolation increased. When I was young and attended meetings, my pulse would hit 150 beats per minute, because one did not know what to expect or what would come next. We could not know what kind of behavior to expect from Saddam through a meeting. Many times one would think that there is no man more noble or generous than Saddam Hussein, but in other situations, he would be mean and spiteful in a way beyond our imagination.

We can think of Saddam's personality as changing over several different phases. First, there was the phase before the invasion of Kuwait; the second phase came after the invasion; then there was the third phase, following the escape of Hussein Kamel in 1995. In the phase prior to Kuwait, his personality was violent and strong, trying to be a famous leader of a nation, not just within Iraq, but throughout the Arab world. As much as he was accomplishing and building in a positive sense, he was a frightening monster to anyone who confronted him, and in the end, this contradicted his long-term objectives. After the invasion of Kuwait, and Iraq's defeat, his personality changed, especially after the revolt of the Shia community in 14 provinces. That was a huge shock to him, because he always thought he had the support of the Iraqi people. What he had created, he had then lost not only the respect, but he lost the trust in his own people, and he became contemptuous of them. He also lost trust in his close, high-ranking generals, the ones close to him, and even close members of his family, because he thought that maybe some of them had involved themselves in the revolution after the invasion of Kuwait.

The next phase was after the escape of Hussein Kamel, and Saddam's elimination of his son-in-law. After that, he became unreasonable, and he isolated himself from the rest of the country. Saddam Hussein would not trust anyone, except for his closest circle. But even within that circle, he would doubt their loyalty, and so he stepped away from them and the government administration. At that point, I was the commander of the Al-Madina [Al-Munawarra] Division and then the corps chief of staff in Tikrit.[40] I remember that he would always move from place to place, always in isolated places. It got to a point where he would not trust his people or any Arab leader, including King Hussein of Jordan. In the past, he had been an active person, visiting the troops on the ground, the various ministries, factories, and other government establishments, and different villages throughout Iraq. In this new phase, he stopped such activity and started requiring the ministers to come to him, and even then only a small number of officials. Some of the ministers had no kind of close, direct contact with Saddam Hussein for almost 2 years. And this goes even for the military leaders. Saddam did not visit his generals, even those of the Republican Guard. Nevertheless, he would request them to come over to him for discussions and meetings.

Saddam Hussein devoted himself to leaving a permanent presence in Iraq's history through the construction of enormous buildings and incredible palaces. He wanted to prove that regardless of the efforts by the Western and other Arab powers to eliminate him, he had left his mark in Iraq.

He also spent much of this time in isolation writing novels, plays, and poetry. He wrote two big stories, in which he used examples from his own life. He titled them "Men around the City" and "Zabiba and the King." You could not understand the effort spent on them! They would play many times in the theaters, and you would be surprised the number of times they played on television. He would not mention that he was the writer of this story or that play, and so unfortunately, most Iraqis had no idea that Saddam was the author. We knew, since we were close to him. In these works he expressed every feeling he had—toward his relations and the problems with his wives, his children, those in his close circles, his people, and his advisors. He expressed what he was going through in those novels.

Here's an interesting story: At the end of 1997 Saddam sent me his personal escort in Tikrit—he was at the Presidential Palace in Tikrit—instructing me to be present along with all the division commanders as soon as possible. I had to be at the palace at a certain time for a top-priority meeting. I suspected there was a conspiracy in the works, like a military coup, or some kind of special duty. It took me some time to gather up all the divisional commanders, who were halfway across the country. I prepared myself and reviewed all the security and defense plans, so that I could brief Saddam if he were to ask me any questions. As I walked in the hall to which he had summoned us, I saw it was full of spectacular individuals; there were all sorts of poets and artists competing with Saddam. I stood there at attention with the other divisional commanders, sitting and waiting for 5 hours ready for his order, without knowing why he had sent for us.

We had no clue about what was going on! Saddam did not speak to us. So there I was thinking all the while that there was going to be a challenging mission, and so I had reviewed all the security plans, thinking there would be a mission for these assembled commanders. I just kept reviewing things and did not listen to any of the poems or anything; I just thought about the plans. Then the soiree ended, and as the poets were leaving and so forth, we went up to Saddam to ask him, "Sir, do you need anything; is there something for us to discuss?" and he just said, "Oh, no. You guys are free to go." And that was it.

On June 30, 2002, I had a discussion with Saddam, and I tried to change the subject to one dealing with a potential future conflict with the Americans. I also talked for 45 minutes, trying to change Iraq's ideology and doctrine of defense to one more like guerrilla warfare, since we were going to lose a conventional war with the Americans. The man listened to me for a full 45 minutes without interruptions. We discussed this issue because we were definitely going to lose the war to the Americans, due to our weak capabilities. Although he disapproved of my suggestion, such matters had never been easy for anyone to approach Saddam—with the possibility of changing our strategy and plans for war.

At the end of his reign, Saddam Hussein became unrealistic. He lived in a fantasy world, where he started saying that God was with him, and that he was an invincible power. He lost confidence in everything—in politics, in Arabs, and in his people—but he had great faith that God would never leave him. Another incident of interest occurred during a meeting with his close ministers where they were talking about the general situation. All of a sudden Saddam lost control and violently pounded his fist on the table, saying, "King Hussein Abu Abdullah [of Jordan], I will never forget that you dragged me into a war, when I was the one who supported you—now you are trying to plan a coup against me?!" Saddam was cursing at King Hussein, and wanted to take revenge against him. Saddam completely diverged from the topic of discussion, and the ministers present and his personal security guards quickly left the room, seeing that he had turned into a monster.

So Saddam's personality caused the loss of a state, the loss of the nation, the loss of a country, the loss of an army, the loss of a party, and the loss of himself.

He made such unrealistic demands and held such stubborn objectives, and then he would try to turn matters into a spiritual issue. His logic was abnormal! He would always say to us, "Preserve the last scene." And indeed, in the last scene he died in extreme courage and heroism: when he was sentenced to death, he defied death and his executioner; he accepted his death sentence. He made sure that at the last moment he went into history standing strong.

What is ironic about this situation is that Saddam always prohibited us from using mobile phones and satellite dishes, but it was just such a prohibited mobile phone that saved his final image. He died as a courageous knight, defying death. He hated these technologies for scientific reasons, but this mobile phone was the thing that confirmed the last scene and preserved what he believed to be his legacy.

Woods: Getting back to the military side, I noticed two things in your description of the 8 years of the Iran-Iraq War. As a professional, you expressed shock in the way the Iranians used the human wave tactics with the Basij charging young men across the minefields. And you show great empathy for these young men, who sacrificed themselves with little chance that their tactic would succeed. Could you give us a picture of what those kinds of attacks were like for the regular Iraqi army, either defensively or offensively? When you came across these masses of militiamen, applying these futile and irrational tactics, what did it look and feel like? Did you see any changes over the course of the 8 years of the war? They were still using the human wave tactics in 1986 and 1987, so was there anything different, or just more of the same?

Hamdani: At the beginning of the Iranian revolution, there was this threat of [the rising] Khomeini. So there was a doctrine that glorified religious scholars. At the beginning of the war and the Iranian Revolution, the Iranian fighters showed a zeal and extreme courage, even where they suffered great losses. A tremendous number of the people had the will to fight and sacrifice themselves, regardless of the costs. With time, however, Khomeini's holiness weakened, and therefore such operations also weakened. The charm of the revolution started to fade in 1985 and 1986. So we can divide the use of human waves into the two periods before and after 1985. In the final stages of the war, it got to the point where the Pasdaran and Basij even started surrendering in large numbers to Iraqi forces. If you compare the will to fight that they had in the first period, it would be 10 times the fervor of what is going on right now in Iraq.

About the mines, we figured that they did not tell their soldiers about these minefields. It seems as if a large percentage of the Iranian officers failed to warn their soldiers about these minefields. We would find Iranian soldiers injured in the fields, and after questioning them about what pushed them to cross the minefield, they would answer that they did not have a clue, that the leader had not told them they were advancing through minefields. Moreover, it appears the Iranian leaders and intelligence kept certain information from the ground forces, because there would be less damage and costs in sending human waves rather than tanks over minefields.

Woods: Did Iraq develop any specific tactics, aside from firepower, to work against this, or was this something that the army had to do nothing to adapt to?

Hamdani: Well, first of all, we increased the minefields. We increased them tenfold so that the Iranians had no chance of crossing the minefields successfully. Say a minefield was 600 meters wide; we would have one mine for every meter. These were the standards of usual minefields. Then, we intensified them in such a way that there were 10 possibilities for a soldier to be injured by a mine along the 600 meters. There would be different kinds of mines: tank mines, vehicle mines, and individual mines—and we started using the Italian bounding mines, which would explode with the maximum amount of damage.[41] We also increased the protection weapons for the minefields, like machineguns. Increased fire would stop the potential for infiltration.

Woods: Another tactical or doctrinal question relates to the fighting around Abadan and Khorramshahr. We have seen some documentary footage of these battles, and we were curious about how well prepared the Iraqi army was to conduct urban operations (in the modern sense of the term) to deal with the population and the complexity of the vertical terrain, the buildings and structures. As these battles were notable for their high intensity, were there any changes between the early fights in Abadan in April 1981 and Khorramshahr that summer? Were there any changes in how the Iranians dealt with them, because at first, they were on the defense, and then in 1982 they came back and pushed the Iraqis out, such as in the case of Khorramshahr and some other small cities? [See figure 4.]

Hamdani: We have to understand that Khorramshahr[42] had a spiritual impact on the Iraqis. These two cities were Iraqi and were given to Iran by the British in recent history. So there was a goal to liberate the occupied Iraqi territories. Many Iraqis saw it as a spiritual duty to return this city to Iraq, as it has always been a symbol of our Iraqi city. It was so important that you could ask anyone within the Iraqi ranks and he would still remember the memo that instructed us to liberate Khorramshahr. It was the general command statement or memo number 99. Everyone would remember this because of its symbolic importance.

At the time, the special forces were of high caliber, as many were graduates of American and Egyptian academies. Therefore, a plan to liberate the city was laid out that relied in particular on Iraqi special forces. To be honest, the Iranians displayed ferocious resistance during the urban fighting, to the point where it became difficult and costly for us to occupy it. They would always attempt to retake

Figure 4. **The southern sector of the war (region of Khorramshahr)**

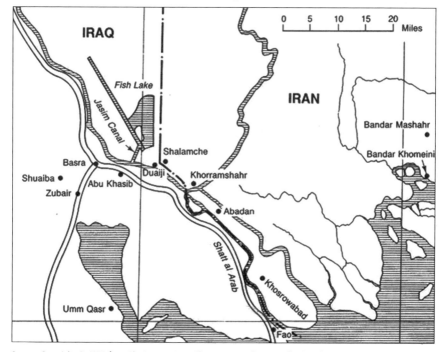

Source: Copyright © 1991 from *The Longest War: The Iran Iraq Military Conflict* by Dilip Hiro. Reproduced by permission of Routledge, Inc., a division of Informa plc. Original map title "The Southernmost War Sector on Land," p. 16.

their last bases even after we had pushed them over the bridge. They would hold every point to the bitter end, so they were able to inflict heavy losses on our forces.

These battles would be difficult for any army, for sure, but the Iranian leadership accepted the heavy losses [their soldiers] suffered, enabling them, through their determination and stubbornness, to regain the territory from us down the road. In the early stage of the war, both armies had high spirits and were at their peak of fighting ability, so there were two stubborn armies fighting each other, each one driven by its own belief [system]. Unfortunately, this caused us to lose the best of our troops, including the special forces, in the first 2 or 3 years of the war. On the other hand, the Iranians also lost the best of their troops in these early stages.

After this, both sides changed their offensive methods to focus more on human masses, pushing people along narrow fronts. For the Iraqis it was especially true in 1986 and 1987. These fronts were small and had a very large number of boots on the ground, leading to massive human massacres. Just as Sun Tzu said, "Battles without strategic planning will turn into human massacres."

Murray: So with most of the special operations forces worn out or destroyed by 1982 on both sides, was the failure to reconstitute this capability a reflection of the huge pressures put on both Iraq and Iran to maintain their extraordinarily large armies, which were expanding throughout the war?

Hamdani: There was an attempt, but it failed because of the lack of time and the continuous demand for forces at the front line. The front could not sustain pulling the troops out to send them for training. And training good units requires a long time. Therefore, the horizontal expansion took place at the expense of the vertical expansion, in terms of building our capabilities. There were high requirements to qualify to be members of the special forces, with its members previously attending the academies of Turkey, Egypt, and the Soviet Union, so the troops we lost were once in a lifetime and were impossible to replace.

Woods: Another thing we would like to hear about are the reasons why the initial Iraqi offensives ended around 19 May 1981. From what you said earlier, it seems like that decision was due to a combination of things, specifically related to some of the actions of the 9th Armored Division, how they had been in an offensive posture with the tanks always out front, but were not moving quickly, and were not doing a lot of reconnaissance. It seems that because they had not done the kinds of preparations necessary to transition to the defense, the initial Iranian counterattacks were effective. Was this the result of the lack of a plan, that there was some idea that Iraq could just go into Iran and hope that certain things would happen, or was it that they would be able to create a new defensive line? It seems like the offense just stopped and nobody transitioned to the defense. Was this due to a lack of planning or a lack of logistics, that the Iraqi army was not able to sustain itself? Why were the Iranian counterattacks so effective?

Hamdani: Well, we failed in our attacks. The Iranians started to take away our territory and attack our troops, so our troops carried out counterattacks to stop them. Most of these attacks failed to push the Iranians out from all locations. The Iranians remained at the borders with those who were killed, and they began to advance into Iraq. There were a few reasons for this. Our main troops were weakened because of the continuous attacks. So while it was possible to provide logistic support, there were many reasons for the failure. The courage of the Iranian soldiers could sustain their losses deep into our territories. And the size of their forces was huge, because they began to gather troops during the attack so they would be superior. So we would not go into Iranian territories anymore, but they could gather any force and achieve success at whatever point they wanted, since they were free to move in their depth. They realized that we no longer had any attack capabilities. Therefore, the Iranians felt safe to move freely and knew that Tehran was secure, and they could gather troops from all their sectors to achieve superiority in whatever specific location they desired to attack. We, on the other hand, had to have defense along the entire border.

Woods: Why were the Iranians so confident that the Iraqi forces would not advance? Was this knowledge of the practical limits of the number of forces Iraq had, and the amount of the logistics the Iraqis could push forward? What was the limiting factor for Iraq at that point in May 1981?

Hamdani: This was a fact of the war. Where could we go, if we wanted to advance to a certain depth in Iran? For example, let us say that as a division commander you wanted to go more than 40 kilometers into Iranian territory, what would be the point? Going this far would not get you any closer to Tehran, because it would still be another 800 kilometers to the Iranian capital. So this imposed a natural limit on the Iraqi offensives. We began to assume a more defensive position. We did not have the capability to push a division 30–40 kilometers into Iran, and such an advance would not have put an end to the war. Our strategy had to become defensive because of the depth of their territory. Cities like Tehran and Isfahan were far too deep in their nation. We knew we no longer had the capability to advance, except using aircraft, which possessed sufficient range.

Discussion Five

1981–1982 Turbulence in Tehran — Iranian Infiltration Tactics — 1982 Attacks around Basra — 1984–1988 Marsh Infiltrations and Iraqi Engineering Efforts — International Support to Iran — Chemical Weapons Usage (Anecdotes, including Halabjah) — Iranian Response to Weapons of Mass Destruction (WMD) — Postwar Preparations with WMD — 1982–1983 Reorganization and Recruiting for Republican Guard — Psychological Support of Saddam to Troops — Postwar Republican Guard Reorganization

Woods: Immediately after the Iraqi offensive culminated and the conflict entered a static period, in 1981 and 1982, it seems there was a significant amount of turbulence in Tehran, precipitated by bombs (car bombs and ordinary explosives), assassinations, and an increase in insurgent activities from organizations like the MEK [Mujahideen-e-Khalq].[43] Do you think that this was the result of Saddam's changing tactics, shifting the battlefield away from the front, or do you think that it was more of a natural occurrence within a revolutionary situation? Or was this just the kind of thing to happen along with the chaos of revolution and war?

Hamdani: Actually, it was not a result of Iraq's actions. It was the result of the nature of matters at hand in Iran—the vast changes occurring in the Iranian political arena, with many of the parties conflicting with the Shah. The Iranian revolution consisted of religious, national, secular, and student currents, all different. But the religious scholars and Khomeini and the components of the religious institutions were better able to drive the revolution forward under the leadership of Khomeini. Of course, there were disputes and competitions among the religious scholars, but Khomeini was able to rise as a leading religious and charismatic personality with his French media presence. So all that happened was a normal part of competing interests during a revolution and a transitional period. On the other hand, the Mujahideen-e-Khalq did carry out the attack at the Islamic conference [office of the Islamic Republic Party] in 1981, which killed 72 people, including Ayatollah Beheshti.[44]

Of course, Iraq had ties with the revolutionary current around Bazargan. The only connection I can think of between Iraq and Iran was with the political party Free Iran. It was a secular party led by Mehdi Bazargan, who held the post as the first prime minister after the revolution.[45]

Khomeini pushed for him to resign from the government, and after that [had him] arrested. Other governments came after that. Ali Raja'i was also killed, and the Minister of Foreign Affairs Sadegh Ghotbzadeh was executed, as he was a CIA [Central Intelligence Agency] agent.[46] There was another politician to come after him called "Omar Shukri Zadeh" [note: the authors can find no public references to this individual] to be the revolutionary minister of foreign affairs, and he was accused of being a CIA spy and then executed. After all this, Iraq started to provide support to MEK.

Woods: You mentioned in several places in your memoirs that one of the most successful things the Iranians did on the tactical battlefront was their infiltration tactics. This is interesting, as it leads us to think about the World War I experience of the Germans. Can you describe the nature of Iranian tactics along the front, especially in the area of the Iraqi IV Corps in early 1982 along the Duwairij River? [See figure 5.]

Hamdani: This was the area of the III and IV Corps, across from the area of what we now call al-Kut, that is, between al-Kut, al-Amara, and the Duwairij River.

The IV Corps was here [northwest of Tib to the south and west of Dehloran], and this was the area of our largest minefield.[47] The area was suitable for armored actions. The majority of the infiltration was by infantry, and there was a large area for gaps. We had the 1st Division in (Dezful) sector, and this was the best route for armor to infiltrate. So we created a large minefield to prevent access to Iranian armor.

The Iranians started to mobilize, since we had taken up strategic defense positions. They began to pull troops from all their sectors and from the depths of their country and put them in a staging area. This process took them about 3 to 5 months. They started the infiltration process at a certain time and in a certain way so they could attack the closest specified front and achieve success in infiltrating by continuously replacing the momentum with more forces. The staging area was at Dezful. We considered that the place where they would gather people from the northern and southern sectors, as well as from deeper in the country. This staging

Figure 5. **Southern war sector**

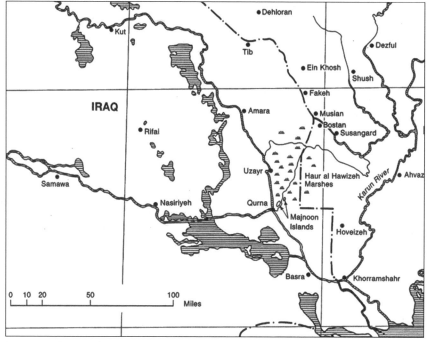

Source: Copyright © 1991 from *The Longest War: The Iran Iraq Military Conflict* by Dilip Hiro. Reproduced by permission of Routledge, Inc., a division of Informa plc. Original map title "The Southernmost War Sector on Land," p. 16.

area gave them the flexibility to assign forces to different parts of the border, while we lacked sufficient manpower to cover the whole border. They attacked from many directions and created a long, drawn-out frontal battle.

Moreover, they had the flexibility to reinforce successful units. If one unit at this point along the border were to penetrate our defenses, they would funnel more people in and keep the momentum going in this direction. There was a good example of this in 1982. They would attack in the form of units, one division at a time, but once they achieved success in one area, the others would retreat back and would join the successful attack.

Woods: Was Iraq able to recognize this operational approach when the Iranians first implemented it? Did the Iraqi 1st Division recognize that Iranian success was coming in the 3d Division sector and reposition its troops accordingly? Was Iraq able to respond to Iran's lateral movements in the early stage of the war?

Hamdani: Well, Iranian infiltration was not deep, because it relied on infantry, and they were only infiltrating during the night. So they could not move more than 10 kilometers at night. The result was limited infiltration. We had to come up with plans for how to contain such attacks [see figure 6].

Figure 6. **General Hamdani's sketch of Iranian infiltration tactics, 1982**

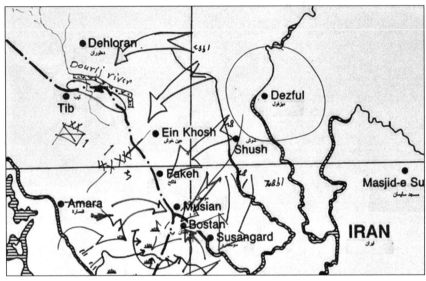

Source: Copyright ©1991 from *The Longest War: The Iran Iraq Military Conflict* by Dilip Hiro. Reproduced by permission of Routledge, Inc., a division of Informa plc. Original map title "The Southernmost War Sector on Land," p. 16. Subsection of map in figure 5 with Hamdani's notations.

The flanking forces would attack on the wings (the flank). This would allow us to reduce and close the penetration the Iranians had made. Approximately 90 percent of Iranian attacks were successful in the early stages, but the attacks invariably lost their momentum. They would seize control of an area, suffering serious losses, and then we would shell them extensively with our artillery and bomb them with air support. But they were very persistent.

The Iranians later realized that they could not achieve success on open ground. So they began to concentrate on the areas that neutralized the movement of our armor and weakened the impact of our air forces and artillery, such as in water-flooded areas, marshes, and sand dunes (and sand bars). In those locations, the impact of our armor and artillery/aerial bombs was less effective. In 1984, the Iranians started to infiltrate the marsh areas, and so our armored elements were not able to get at them because of the water and high vegetation.

Murray: Did this represent an effort by the Iranians to wage and sustain a long-term war of attrition to wear down Iraq until it finally broke?

Hamdani: Yes, this played a role after 1984, when they concentrated on valleys and rough mountain areas, where it was difficult for our armor to move. This was the turning point, where they adopted new tactics toward the end of 1984. They were superior in infantry, while we were superior in armor, and so they neutralized our armor in this fashion.

Woods: You described the Iranian operations around Basra [tactically suicidal attacks] in the summer of 1982 as "mad." What was different about Basra? Did the Iranians think that being the second Iraqi city, that if they could break into and capture Basra, then maybe they would be able to break Saddam's regime? What was different about the way Iran attacked Basra?

Hamdani: The land east of Basra, in general, has a large open area suitable for armored units, and so we easily repulsed the Iranian attacks by our armor, before they could make it to the Shatt al-Arab and al-Basateen areas.[48]

Murray: As the Iranians spent significant time focusing on Basra, with this open terrain that favored Iraq, why wasn't there a greater emphasis in the north to break through to Baghdad, where the mountains would favor the infantry? Was it a matter of logistics?

Hamdani: In fact, all the roads leading to Baghdad are in open areas that favor armored troops and air forces, and the Republican Guard and other ground forces would have provided a great obstacle to the Iranians. So they did not think they would succeed in getting to Baghdad. This meant that their main effort aimed at [making gains in] the south. Moreover, they preferred Basra for several reasons: the majority of the population there is Shi'ite, and in terms of the entire Gulf region, Iraq has a strategic location. If Iran were able to occupy Basra and turn it into an emirate or an independent government separate from Iraq (it would be a part of Muhammarah, Arabistan, Ahwaz, and so forth), they would cut off Iraq from the Gulf. So we can see they had strategic interests in this area.

The idea of protecting Basra from Iranian incursions goes back to the Shah's era, and is the reason why Iraq's leaders had constructed the Fish Lake in the mid-1970s. The lake was a barrier to the Iranian armored troops. It was intended to limit their movement and the potential for a strategic long-term effort to take over Basra. The Iraqi National Defense Plan was prepared before Saddam took power to address the potential for the Iranian 90th Armored Division to attack and occupy Basra. At that time [early 1970s], we had fewer armored units, and those we did have were focusing on moving into Jordan [to support an Arab war against Israel]. Thus, we built this water barrier to limit the possibility of an Iranian attack on this front. We studied this plan in the staff college and war college in the mid and late 1970s. It was always a part of the Iraqi defense line.

In 1982, an Iranian armored division began infiltrating in this area and attacked along two axes—one in this area, and then one farther south. Because of the open terrain farther north and closer to Baghdad, the Iraqi army intercepted the Iranians. The Iranians then started working their way south, trying to find another way to infiltrate. So it was not until late 1982 that they actually came across the Fish Lake and destroyed our 9th Division. Despite this Iranian success, our armored troops were able to launch attacks in these directions.

As of 1984, they moved to the marsh areas north of the lake and the Maj-nun Islands [see figure 5]. And their infantry operated well down in this area. They learned the lesson in 1982 that they could not be successful in the open areas both east of Basra and east of Amara [see figure 4]. After 1987, they began a strategy of attrition aimed at our armored forces and air force—the influence of our air force remained limited because of the soft land and water in these areas.

Woods: With all these operations around the marshes and lake areas, engineers had their work cut out for them. Both Iraqi and Iranian engineers had to develop new methods. For Iraq's engineers, you have described them as building "fingers of land" and artificial sand bars. Iranian engineers focused on building small pontoon bridges and moving them quickly. Can you describe some of this engineer effort and the fighting environment?

Hamdani: One thing that the Iranians relied upon was using hovercraft for infantry movements. They connected one area to another by using bridges made out of a cork material, which would float on the water. They also made small rafts out of the same material to float artillery inside the rivers [like an artillery barge].

There were also engineering efforts in the oil areas, where they built "dirt stoppers" [berms]. They occupied these areas and expanded them with the [cork material] because the longest of the reed plants was 3 meters. They were able to build combat bases for their soldiers on the berms in our oil fields, which they expanded with the cork. Elevated dirt roads connected the oil fields and refineries to one another. The height of the reed plants made reconnaissance difficult to the point where we could not see what the enemy was doing, for example, when the Iranians set up their floating artillery positions. We had to build high observation posts and begin using our helicopters in different ways, to fly at certain elevations in order to get a better view. Such operations lasted from 1984 to 1988.

We had a hard time maneuvering our Republican Guard troops [in this area], and used amphibious forces and engineering troops, as well as amphibious armor such as the BMP–1 and BMP–2. We also relied on our helicopters for dropping our airborne units in different locations for our counterattacks. And during this time, we used chemical weapons extensively.

Murray: It appears that as the war went on the Iraqis resupplied and upgraded their tanks and equipment, such as with the T–72s, while the Iranians were getting no new tanks during the war. Therefore as their tanks were destroyed and not replaced, they became a lighter and lighter force, dependent on their infantry. Is this the case?

Hamdani: Yes, this is correct. They had to switch from a heavy to a light army because of their nonreplacement.

Moreover, the Iranians relied on the expertise of the North Koreans. As a result, their engineering methods, as far as tactical bridges and floating bridges and pipelines they built on the Shatt al-Arab, all came from the Korean experts who worked with them. Iran received military support and advice from North Korea as well as the Pakistanis, the latter especially for the air force, but the most came from the North Koreans. This was the source of many of their military innovations during the war. But this was not government-sponsored support. It only came from volunteers who pretended to be war experts. The Iranians would only take advice directly from Shi'i Pakistanis.[49]

Woods: Changing the subject a bit, it seems that the most glaring topic absent from your memoir is a discussion of chemical weapons and their effectiveness. Why is it that you left WMD out? Was it because of the environment in which you were writing, which was not conducive to describing weapons of mass destruction or chemical weapons of any kind? Beyond this, I would also like to get your impression, as a professional officer, of the implications of using chemical weapons on the battlefield. Obviously, it could be used against you, and it is clearly dangerous to handle. And it works both ways; the wind could change or you might have to maneuver across a contaminated battlefield. Could you describe for us the chemical warfare in the war, especially its early use in 1983 and 1984?

Hamdani: Well, I referred to chemical weapons as "Special Weapons" [in the final published version of the memoirs, not the draft available to the Project 1946 team]. On April 17, 1988, Iraqi artillery units launched more than 1,000 firings (all types of artillery fire), and in this, I believe, the bombardment used chemical weapons. It was a mix of artillery, tanks, rockets, and all this, including, I believe, chemical weapons.[50] Meanwhile, the wind did change direction, and this forced our units to continue wearing the masks. Even the Republican Guard Headquarters was slightly affected [by the Iraqi chemicals]. And this is in the more updated published version of my memoirs.

Woods: At some point in 1983, you became the commander of an armor unit; could you describe for us what it was like for you when you first found out Iraq was going to use chemical weapons? Was the purpose of the chemical weapons in your mind to provide a tactical solution?

Hamdani: We feared the effects of the chemical weapons on ourselves because of the wind. The problem we had was that when our soldiers wore their protective masks, it would also limit their combat effectiveness, and the masks were generally uncomfortable. In the case of the wind changing directions, it would strike us, and we had to continue fighting while wearing the protective masks.

We hoped that the attacks would go deep, not just at the front line. We wanted to use the chemical attacks on the Iranian reserves in depth, so that we could fight more freely. We requested that headquarters use the chemical weapons on the supply lines inside Iran.

In this last war, in 2003, I asked Saddam Hussein whether he was planning to use chemical weapons or not, so that I would know how to plan.[51] He answered,

"No, there is no use for that." So I deployed my troops more flexibly without having to worry about the possible use of chemical weapons. My belief that we would not use chemical weapons was reinforced by the fact that we were going to fight in populated areas like the countryside and villages. Moreover, from my perspective, the impact of the use of chemicals is more psychological than material.

Another example was in the battle of Halabjah, in 1987, the 84th Iranian Infantry Division and the 55th Iranian Parachute Brigade were both present. The target in Halabjah was not the Kurds, but these two units.

Woods: Can you describe the [military] decision process when the chemical weapons were used during the war?

Hamdani: There was a special higher headquarters established for the use of such weapons, not only at the field level but also at the strategic and operational levels, to plan for chemical attacks. The Iraqi army artillery commander would be at this headquarters at a senior level, and the chemical commander would also always be a member of this headquarters. The officer in charge would be the Iraqi army's operations director.

Murray: Was the decision to use chemical weapons a measure of desperation, or was it an attempt to escalate the war as a means to persuade the Iranians to stop the war?

Hamdani: Both. It was an "and," not an "or." To make up for the troops we lacked, we required greater artillery capability. For example, we used chemical weapons in the lower Fao area, since the land comprises soft soil and marshes, which rendered our artillery and air-delivered weapons useless and prevented the effective employment of armor. For these reasons, the Iranians occupied and defended these areas, where air attacks or armored support would not have a great impact. Therefore, we had no other choice but to use the chemical weapons. We used the chemicals in Al-Huwayzah area, in Majnun, and in Shalamjah [Chalamjeh], the orchard area.

This entire area is soft. The Iranians started to pay great attention to Al-Fao Island, and they defended it with extreme resistance after they failed to occupy Basra. After the Iranians realized how strong Iraqi defenses around Basra were, they started moving south, and attacked areas such as the island areas—Bubyan, for example. These islands are full of palm trees and so forth. They attacked and crossed at Ma'amer (along the Fao Peninsula), and the port of Al-Fao. In the area that the Iranians occupied, we had stationed the 26th Division. The Iranians planned another attack, pretending that they would attack the 7th Division. The moment they attacked, they took over the southern tip of Fao, and then started working their way north along the "Strategic Road." This road continues up to Um-Qasr. But our troops were able to gain control of the attack in this location and then began to launch counterattacks.[52]

Woods: Is this one of the cases where you used chemical weapons close to the front, or where you tried to use it deep—on the logistics and crossing areas?

Hamdani: No, this is where we settled down and pushed the Iranians to this other location, across a canal. The Iranians struggled desperately in this location and displayed tremendous resistance. Then they received backup support from their artillery, and after 2 months of fighting they had stopped our forces at this point along the canal. This is when the attack with the chemicals took place. The operations took place in 1986, and we also launched a chemical attack in 1988, the year of liberation, when we finally pushed them out of this area. In 1988, the Republican Guard was heavily involved in the liberation. The number of soldiers we lost [killed in action] from 1986–1988 was 53,000, and we had 220,000 injured. So that's why we used chemicals, when such battles happened, because the losses were unbearable.

In Halabjah, in 1987, the Iranians had two divisions, the 84th Iranian Division and the 55th Parachute (Airborne) Division. The Iranians entered Halabjah near the area of Darbandikhan Lake, and the dam, which has a high elevation. They occupied this area and moved to take the Shadiran Mountain, after which the land becomes flat all the way to Sulaimaniyah. So if they succeeded in getting past Shadiran Mountain, they would be able to infiltrate much more and reach Sulaimaniyah. Our defensive line here was desperate and relying especially on our special forces.

The Kurds in Halabjah had evacuated. They left because the battle had been going on for over a month before the use of chemicals. Jalal Talabani controlled the eastern sector, and the Iraqi government contacted him, as it had become an operational area, fearing for the safety of the Kurdish residents [and warned them] not to stay in the area. Talabani notified [the Iraqi] command that the Kurds had evacuated the area. To my knowledge, he signed a document confirming that the evacuation took place from the village.

Then, we used the artillery to launch chemicals on this sector. The attack almost entirely exterminated the Iranian division. This was the first true mass use of chemicals, where the air force fully exterminated the 84th Division. It was limited to Halabjah Valley. This had a tremendous psychological effect on the rest of the Iranian soldiers. This is not meant to be a defense of what we did, but for the purposes of historical honesty, the Kurds were not the target of this attack. We had focused it on the Iranian forces present in that area. The Kurds who died during that attack were those folks who refused to obey orders to evacuate the city, and their numbers did not exceed 75–150 killed.[53] And another thing is that the Iranians also retaliated by using chemical weapons.

Murray: It seems that the Iranians did not use the chemical weapons until the very end of the war. Why?

Hamdani: It was their lack of capabilities and limited production. They only had a limited capability when we started using chemical weapons, not to mention all the effort to produce those.

Woods: What do you think the Iranians learned through all this 8 years of experience about chemical weapons? What did Iran take away from that experience?

Hamdani: Well, they had countermeasures, for sure. For example, they developed some kind of distilled gases that looked like white smoke to minimize the effects of a chemical attack. POWs told us of these tools, but we were never able to find out what it was that they were using, and our specialists could not come to any conclusion about the substance the Iranians were using.

Woods: I'd like to hear about how you used your experience fighting the Iranians in the 1980s in your senior staff positions in the early 1990s, and finally your corps command in the late 1990s. How did your thoughts about and plans for fighting Iran develop over time? Did you expect that Iran would use chemicals? Apparently, Iraq did not have chemicals in the late 1990s, but I presume you thought Iran did. After all, they used them in the late 1980s, and were not under the same restrictions as Iraq was after the 1991 war. Did you anticipate or expect the Iranians to use chemical weapons, had you gone to war in the 1990s, based on what they had learned fighting in the 1980s?

Hamdani: In the 1990s, for the most part, we had a lot of good protection equipment, more than what the Iraqi army needed, and so our army was trained and each soldier was provided with two [chemical] protection masks that fit his size. Our soldiers had also received training in case of chemical attacks. And we had decontamination stations in each brigade, and in the headquarters of the battalions and companies. The picture that was shown in Colin Powell's presentation[54] was actually a picture of a decontamination station of the 14th Brigade inside part of the Medina Munawwara Division. So yes, there was always the assumption that had we gone to war after 1991, Iran would have used chemical weapons.

Woods: Let us go back to the Iran-Iraq War. You have described the period of October-November 1982 as a quiet one. At around this time [the Republican Guard] was being issued new equipment. You were given command of the Hamza Battalion just as it took possession of brand-new T–72s. Saddam Hussein directed that a series of large-scale tests and training exercises be conducted in early 1983. These were to be followed by a period of analyzing the lessons. Can you describe what happened in this period? How were the Republican Guard forces pulled back away from the front, reorganized, expanded, and given new equipment? Can you describe this process, and specifically Saddam's involvement? Did the "lessons learned" process aim to adjust current doctrine?

Hamdani: I came to command the Republican Guard Battalion (Hamza) as a result of the battle of Al-Hindidi. In that battle, my battalion had performed in outstanding fashion. Saddam used to rely on his relatives' Republican Guard battalions, but his relatives were not disciplined and had little competence and only limited previous participation in war. So Saddam began to choose commanders from the best Iraqi armored battalions to command Republican Guard battalions, whereas previously he had chosen only his relatives.

Obviously, Saddam had started to realize that the [overall] capabilities of the Iraqi army were weakening; even the competent troops were starting to lose. Moreover, at this point, Saddam finally recognized that this was going to be a longer war than he had expected. So he started picking the best officers, commanding officers, and junior officers within the Iraqi army and put them in the Republican Guard, and he aimed to save this new force for the major counterattack, as frontline forces were weakening day by day. This was in line with the recommendations of the general officers to create a special armored force that was well equipped and well trained, led by expert, high-ranking officers, with great experience, and to use this force on special occasions to counterattack serious threats.

Murray: The great British soldier of World War II, Lord Slim, argued that the creation of large specialized forces had a negative tendency on the remainder of British forces, and that, in fact, it would have been better to aim for a higher overall standard throughout the Fourteenth Army than create special forces. This was clearly not the approach of the German and Soviet armies in World War II, where they had a relatively small percentage of elite guard divisions or SS units with all the best equipment, leaving the rest with relative junk. In Iraq's case, do you feel this was a wise decision, or should the emphasis have been more on raising the standards of the whole army?

Hamdani: Well, in general, around the world, the majority of the world's armies rely on two or three types of troops of different types. Even the United States has the National Guard for every state, but also the Marines, who are specialized for special operations. And the presence of the Marines does not reduce the importance of the National Guard. There is a difference in the kind of assignment that each force takes on. For example, at this time, the regular army would undertake ground offensives, and they would go to the objective but would stop, as it was a done deal when they reached their target. On the other hand, the Republican Guard would conduct several operations, moving from up in the north down to the south and from the east to the west through several battles, and would probably resist more effectively than the regular army because of their better training and mentality.

Every time I led a mission, I would tell my soldiers that failure was not an option, that they must win the battle, for there were no forces behind them, only traffic police. With this mentality, there were no options, and it was different from the regular army soldiers. We would have great momentum, a strong attack, and a clear goal with well-developed plans, because we would always know that we were the last line, and that we would lose if we turned back.

Murray: Was it an all-volunteer force of both officers and soldiers, or were entire Republican Guards units hand selected? How did the political reliability of the Republican Guard officers during this period play a role? Obviously after the war was over, political reliability would come back as a major influence.

Hamdani: The selection process for how the Republican Guard chose its officers was that [its recruiters] picked the experienced and qualified officers from the original army. And the loyalty issue was more of a psychological state, since members of the Republican Guard Army felt that Saddam Hussein was their direct leader. Saddam held a certain position in the leadership for the Republican Guard, who felt that they had a different chain of command and that they had open communication and direct contact with Saddam. So they saw him as taking care of their interests. It gave the psychological impression that they were important and affected the fashion with which they carried themselves and conducted their operations during battle.

Woods: You have described Saddam as having dialogues with fairly low-level commanders and, especially after 1985, with brigade and division commanders of the Republican Guard. Tell us some more about this.

Hamdani: Well, this would provide significant psychological import, because Saddam would not meet with the chief of staff of the army or the minister according to the chain of command. Thus, the soldier would feel that Saddam was talking to him directly, regardless of the loyalty or the party affiliation. But this was just a psychological effect, like, for instance, President Bush somewhere talking to a soldier, as if he were a friend, cheering him up. So regardless of what the soldier might think of Saddam, the direct contact had an impact on him. This shows the difference between the Republican Guard and regular army loyalties and behavior.

Throughout the war and afterward, most Iraqi officers started to realize that they did not want to become members of the Republican Guard, because of the great responsibility demanded of them. There were approximately 365 days worth of training, with high-level missions, and high levels of expectations and sacrifices from the Republican Guard. It was all psychological.

Murray: When the war with Iran was over, was there an effort to bring the regular army up to the standards of the Republican Guard, or was it simply to continue along the same track that had existed during the war, with the Republican Guard holding the elite spot, and the regular army at a lower level?

Hamdani: In fact, after the war they tried to reorganize the entire Iraqi army and Republican Guard to lower the number of soldiers. We had about 37 divisions when we started the war and that was up from 11 divisions originally. During the war, we increased the army up to 57 divisions. So this definitely consumed the society's manpower, and it did not seem appropriate for the army to continue in this way. Therefore, the process of reducing the army's size and developing lessons learned from the war started in 1989, but then the Kuwait crisis changed the matter, and the same forces demolished after the Iran-Iraq War were called back again, but with less spirit, of course.

Murray: The Israeli Army specifically used its initial elite unit, the Golani, as an example of the level to which they wanted to train up their infantry forces. In 1973, when the U.S. Army created the Ranger Regiment, it was deliberately created as an elite force, but also to set the standard for the whole of the army's infantry. Was there any kind of conception, in terms of the 1980 reforms, that the Republican Guard was going to serve as an example for what the rest of the force should be, or was it still conceived of as a two-tier force?

Hamdani: The Republican Guard remained as the model of high standards for the Iraqi army, of the well trained and experienced forces that had existed in the 1970s, as evidenced by their engagements with Israel. Therefore, Iraqi leaders tried to use this as the standard for the rest of the army. For example, when I took command of the Al-Madina Al-Munawwarah division in the Republican Guard, I was always trying to bring its soldiers back to the high level of expectations that I had as commander of the 3ᵈ Division, because that was the best army division in the region. Personally, as a division commander and later as a corps commander, I used to stay up at night in order to review the level of the training tests, the training methods developed for the soldiers and the officers, and the level of threat that we were going to face. I would spend hours focusing on how to learn from our prior battles, such as with Israel, and how this should affect our training programs. We always tried to set the bar high for the special forces, at the level of the Israeli Army, and then, once we got to know U.S. forces, we tried to set our bar to the level of the Russian and U.S. Special Forces. These were our goals, we always tried to improve everything, and this all had a significant impact.

I used to ask the commanders, the division and brigade commanders, after showing them a picture I had of American soldiers standing all straight in their uniforms next to a convoy. I would then compare that depiction to a picture of regular Iraqi officers, asking them, "Can you explain to me why the Iraqi soldier looks this way, while the American soldier looks that way? One of them [the Iraqi] looks disappointing, while the other [American] one is standing there, confident and proud, with his Kevlar looking great." I even told Saddam Hussein this and commented: "The training, preparation level, and discipline of the soldiers should be this [the American] way."

Murray: This is interesting, because it is clear that Saddam did not believe that discipline was important. To him, the essential thing was the "warrior spirit" and the "warrior will," not the sense that, in fact, discipline was far more important. Often the "warrior spirit" gets you killed, while discipline kills the other person.

Hamdani: True. This is because Saddam was never a military officer.

Discussion Six

Summer 1983 Iranian Offensive into Haj Umran—Northern Mountain Operations and Kurdish Support—A 1,000-kilometer Front—Threats to the Dams and Baghdad—Unpredictable Iranian Strategy and Tactics—February 1984 Iraqi 6th Armored Division Losses—Iranian Marsh Operations—Intelligence Development and Satellite Support in March 1985

Woods: The Iranian offensive into the Haj Umran sector in July-August of 1983 was considered one of the most significant threats to Baghdad early in the war. Because of this offensive, you essentially had to evacuate sectors in the south and in some cases airlift reinforcements directly into the fight in the north. Can you describe these movements for us? [See figures 7 and 8.]

Hamdani: When the Iranians realized they were unable to achieve success in the areas of Iraqi superiority in armored and air force units, particularly in the south, they altered their strategy from one of seeking deep penetrations to one of mounting operations in areas of complex terrain, where the use of armored and air force units was difficult. So they started to work in the mountain and marsh areas to achieve a greater degree of success. [In the north] they also found Kurdish parties who cooperated with them, such as the PUK [Patriotic Union of Kurdistan] and the KDP [Kurdish Democratic Party]. [In the south], they had the Iraqi Da'wa party, which was loyal to Iran.

Woods: Can you describe specifically what the PUK and the KDP did to provide support? Was it close cooperation, or were they acting as covering forces? How specifically did Kurdish forces act in concert with the Iranian offensive?

Hamdani: They provided three types of help. First, they offered guidance on the unfamiliar terrain and information about the region; second, they helped in matters of logistics; and third, they participated along part of the front line with small teams of Iranians, because of their knowledge of the area.

This Iranian tactic of collaborating with dissident Iraqi groups caused Iraqi forces to disperse from the south to the north and stretched our line of defense. This forced the Iraqi leaders to confront major battles on two fronts, separated by a considerable distance.

Woods: The reports in the Western press at the time suggest that this battle [Haj Umran sector in July-August of 1983] was the first major use of chemicals by Iraq, and it resulted from a lack of sufficient forces.[55] Was the use of chemicals at this point to help the Iraqi forces buy time to reposition?

Hamdani: Well, I do not think that this was the first time. No chemical weapons were used in 1983. The first time we used them, it happened later, maybe in 1986 and afterward, but nothing during this earlier period.[56]

We have to understand that in the early stages of the war, there was an agreement between the Kurdish leadership of the PUK and KDP with the central Iraqi government. Saddam's regime allowed them legally not to participate in the conflict. They would have to be members of the army to fight the Iranians. Unfortunately, they stabbed Saddam in the back by providing support for the Iranians in the early stages of the war. Saddam considered this action as the first act of treason by the Kurds toward the central government.

Murray: What do you think the Iranian aim was in launching this late 1983 offensive? Was the offensive aimed to pull the Iraqi forces out of the south, or did it have some major operational goal such as pushing on to Baghdad? Do you think they were simply fighting the war of exhaustion against Iraq by trying to extend the battlefront, or were they fighting a much larger sort of operation, literally aiming to knock Saddam's regime out of power?

Hamdani: In fact, there were many reasons. One was to compensate for their losses and failures in several attacks in the center and the south. There was considerable pressure coming from Khomeini on the regular army and militia for their

Figure 7. **Iranian *Dawn* offensives—northern sector, 1983–1986**

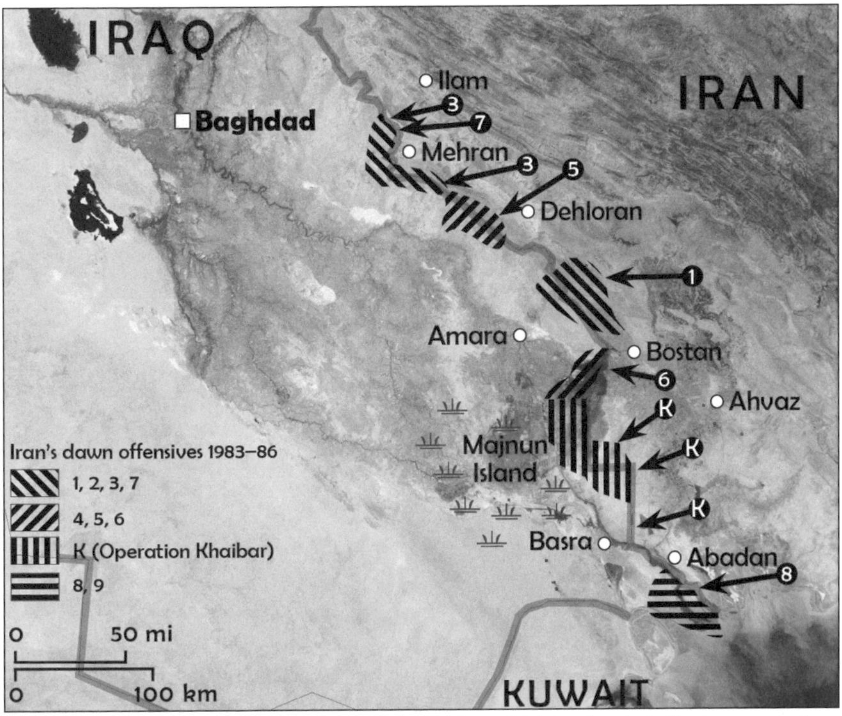

Source: Satellite image courtesy of National Aeronautics and Space Administration. Available at <www.parstimes. com/spaceimages/mideast/>.

failures at the time. So they responded in this way to show strength to the political and religious leadership.

Another reason was to force the Iraqi leadership to fight over two fronts separated by almost 1,000 kilometers. It is difficult for any military to fight on fronts separated by this kind of distance. This brings up the expression known to military officers of "maneuvering on interior lines." Take Israel, for example. It is not difficult for the Israelis at the strategic level, because they can maneuver at the interior lines, where at one point they would move against Egypt and then at another toward Syria.

Another reason was to gain an area where the Iranians might form a provisional government in the future. If the northern area was suitable and the mountain areas had Kurdish parties that were a part of the Iraqi government, it would be possible for the Iranians to occupy this area and establish an independent state. This would create internal political conflicts for the central Iraqi government.

Woods: This sounds like the strategy the Shah used in the 1974–1975 Kurdish war, correct?

Figure 8. **Iranian *Dawn* offensives—central and southern sectors, 1983–1986**

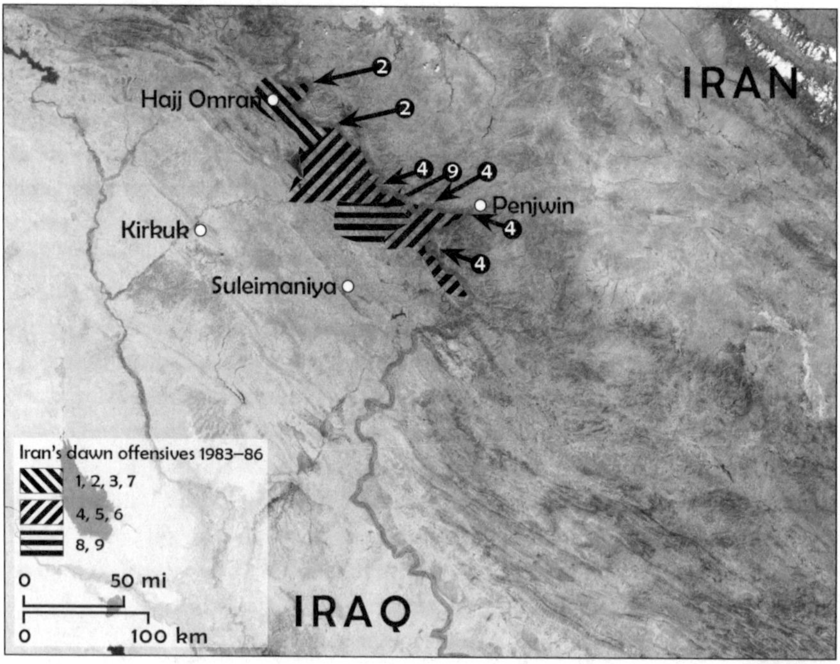

Source: Satellite image courtesy of National Aeronautics and Space Administration. Available at <www.parstimes.com/spaceimages/mideast/>.

Hamdani: Yes. The other issue is that mountainous areas require a large number of troops, and therefore would consume a major part of Iraq's reserves. This would hurt the effectiveness of the remainder of the force down south.

Murray: Was it not also advantageous to the Iranians to open a front here because it was logistically easier to supply from Tehran and the centers of Iranian power, rather than the fighting in the south?

Hamdani: Yes, I agree. But we have to remember that the Kurds provided logistic support that was already in place in the mountains.

The other critical danger that concerned the central government of Iraq, and that Saddam worried about, was that if Iranian forces made it to the dams of the rivers in the north, they would gain a major advantage. Those dams were critical, because if the Iranians were to destroy them, the central and southern areas [of Iraq] would be flooded. From the Iranian perspective, this would represent a great achievement. On the other hand, at this time, there was never a direct threat to Baghdad.

Woods: Can you tell us more about the Iranian offensive that began on 21 February 1984? Your memoirs described these attacks as occurring across the whole sector around Basra and just to the north of Basra, but the Iranian tactics were "very unclear." What do you mean by this? What was it about the Iranian tactics that was unclear?

Hamdani: Well, as to how the Iranians were operating, the majority of the people giving commands were not a part of a centralized command structure. As I mentioned earlier, there were multiple lines connected to Ayatollah Khomeini, regular lines of the regular armies, the Pasdaran militias, and the Basij volunteers. Everyone connected to Ayatollah Khomeini, and they competed amongst themselves, as to who would have more influence on the front to attack the Iraqis and damage Saddam. Their operations were not coordinated on the ground, and so, for a while, when we analyzed their movements, we could not make any sense of what they were doing. We were trying to figure out what was going on, and finally we realized that each one of these units was operating independently, and that there was no C^2, no strategic planning.

Woods: So in the Iraqi staff, you were looking at all this and saying, "What is their plan, what is their strategy?"

Hamdani: We kept doing analyses, and one of the combat patrols sent to one of the valleys clashed with a hostile patrol. I decided personally to investigate [by interrogating] a prisoner. (There were five of them, but four were killed.) The one [Iranian] who survived had a camera and a tape of their missions. He had traveled from deep in Iran over the previous days and weeks. We interrogated him and looked at the tape. It showed the five militia members in the area of Isfahan, with a sheikh or an imam. Then it showed them moving along the road in a civilian vehicle toward the front. So I had him clarify to me how his patrol came all the way from Isfahan to Iraq directly, despite all the preexisting Iranian military formations and divisions.

He told me that he was a follower of so-and-so Husayniyah [name of a local imam] and that he and his men had received the mission to go to the front and reach Karbala. Their entire group consisted of approximately 30 militants from Isfahan. I asked him how did he cross the battle line into this sector, and he asked me, "What line?" He said he had come to cross in this location because this was the area of operations of a commander who had ties to his imam. So when they got to the front line, he said, it was the duty of the [Iranian soldiers] there to let [him and his fellow soldiers] execute their mission and then come back. This kind of thing never happened before in any army in the world.

This local imam formed a force that moved approximately 700 kilometers directly from Isfahan to the front line. From a military perspective, this is a sense-less suicide . . . to try to send these men all the way to Karbala.

Woods: I would like to understand a little more about the losses suffered by the 6th Armored Division in operations during February 1984. You describe in your memoirs the difficulties the 6th Armored Division had in the [central front] marshes, and that they suffered heavy losses. Can you describe Iranian and Iraqi armored operations in and around the marsh area? Is there anything aside from the engineering improvements, already discussed, that can help us understand how Iraqi armor operated in this area? Can you describe what sort of mechanized operations the Iranians pursued?

Hamdani: The Iranians surprised the Iraqis at the beginning of the fight, because we considered the area of Baneh [note: location name unclear] to be well protected by Iraqi defenses. The defenders relied on natural and artificial barriers in that sector, such as minefields and other kinds of physical obstacles. The negligence of Iraqi leaders at that time lay in the fact that they thought the enemy would not cross these depressions and marshes, and, therefore, they actually reduced their defenses. So the Iranian attack [on the 6th Armored Division] was a surprise. That was the first problem.

The second was that the Iranians deployed a well-trained and equipped infantry division. They deployed an effective resistance in this area that was hard to operate in and maneuver around. Before the attack, they launched a small mission that did not catch our attention. They used frogmen to explore the approaches to our positions. Some of the [Iranian] divers were killed or injured, but this did not affect the Iraqi front. This was a huge mistake on the part of the commanders in the area for not paying attention and realizing this reconnaissance mission was clearly part of a larger plan.

Woods: You mention in your memoirs that "to prevent further losses, the commander of the 6th Armored Division took the responsible decision to withdraw. He courageously accepted the consequences of his actions." Can you explain what this means? Was he forced out of command or removed by Saddam? What happened to the 6th Armored commander who had responsibilities for that sector?

Hamdani: Yes, I will explain the answer to this question, but this is part of a broader issue that I must explain along the way.

This commander was courageous, realistic, and professional. I participated and fought alongside him in this battle, so I speak from experience. Due to the defeat, he lost his command and received an assignment as the planning officer for 2 months, after which he went into retirement. This was not the appropriate way to compensate him for what he had done and for all his experience.

The corps commander, who gave this mild, unexpected punishment, General Maher 'Abd Rashid, was stupid, but he was a close friend of Saddam Hussein. The division commander told me that I was probably only one of a few commanders who came back to thank him and express gratitude for his long service in the regular army. The defeat of the division was not due to the 6th Division commander's mistakes. It was the mistakes of the corps commander, General Maher 'Abd Rashid, which had resulted in the great losses on the ground and allowed the Iranians to surprise us. Earlier, the Iranians were also able to surprise us on Bubyan, 30 kilometers south of Basra. The corps commander saw this attack, which came just before the main attack on the 6th Division, as though it [the Bubyan attack] was going to be the main thrust. So the Iranians tricked the corps commander, not the division commander, into sending his reserves in this direction. Then the enemy infiltrated through the marshes [and hit the 6th Division]. They launched a powerful and skillful infiltration with boats, helicopters, and various engineering units for airlift and artillery [see figure 9].

Woods: Were there any issues at this point with the marsh Arabs and the various tribes?

Hamdani: Well, there was not much of a population, just small groups of people who were fishermen, and they did not have much influence. But back to the battle. The Iranians crossed the marsh and reached all the way to the Tigris River. Thanks to their engineering efforts, beyond any imagination, and their great level of tolerance and courage, the Iranians were able at this phase to develop their defenses in that area in such a way that, in just a few weeks, they built these tactical bridges and pontoons [Hamdani describes them as "cork" bridges], and expanded some of the dirt berms. It was really an incredible feat of engineering. At the same time, our forces, including the 6th Division were unable to counterattack into the marsh areas. So the 6th Armored Division decided to withdraw its troops rather than sacrifice one of Iraq's best divisions.

Woods: Did Iraqi intelligence ever pick up on the engineering preparations and the buildup of the Iranian bridging teams?

Figure 9. **Bubyan and Shatt al-Arab**

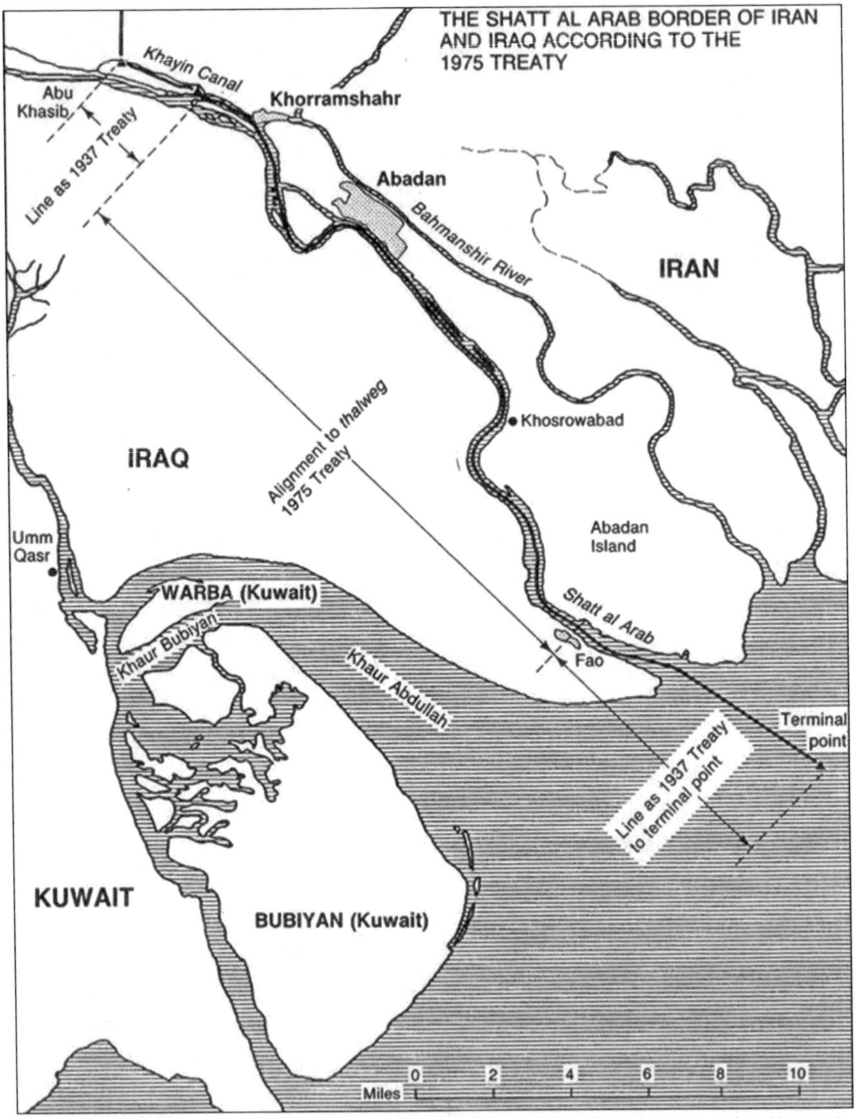

THE SHATT AL ARAB BORDER OF IRAN AND IRAQ ACCORDING TO THE 1975 TREATY

Source: Copyright © 1991 from *The Longest War: The Iran Iraq Military Conflict* by Dilip Hiro. Reproduced by permission of Routledge, Inc., a division of Informa plc. Original map title "The Shatt Al Arab Border of Iran and Iraq According to the 1975 Treaty," p. 12.

Hamdani: In fact, we were taken by surprise. There were many problems because of a lack of intelligence. The other thing is that we did not expect that Iranians, or any army for that matter, could survive for more than a week in the marshes. But the Iranians proved their capacity to persist by living with the fish and foxes, and so forth. They really surprised everybody.

Even using our air units and helicopters, we were not successful because of the type of plants and the terrain. I mean the high grass and reeds grew to a height of 3 meters. We also lost the value of our air support in the marshes. Moreover, it was difficult for ground radar to intercept enemy movements, because when the wind blew and moved the plants, it created all sorts of sounds, and the radar screens would become fuzzy. So because of this phenomenon, we could detect only the sounds of engines, such as on a large boat, but not the sounds of people.

Murray/Woods: It seems a couple of things are going on here. One is Iraqi commanders underestimating Iranian tenacity, as well as the growing sophistication, perhaps, among the Iranians to take advantage of the terrain in order to minimize Iraqi capabilities. This is a different kind of operation occurring in the marshes than what was going on with the imam sending the patrol from Isfahan to Karbala.

Hamdani: That's right; this was well organized and well planned. The truth is that the Iranians displayed a high level of performance, and different capabilities, such as the engineering, even with the large numbers of losses within their forces. I must have seen about 50 bodies floating in the river in the marshes, and these were regular Iranian army, not the militia. They were not concerned with losses or choosing the front, and, unfortunately, they never cared about their fallen soldiers. You would see them being grabbed and eaten by fish, and the Iranians would just leave them dying.

Woods: You mentioned the lack of high-quality intelligence. In your memoirs, you make a specific note that not long after this, in March of 1985 with the Taj al-Ma'arek battle, there was an improvement in intelligence. You mentioned satellite pictures and that sort of thing. So it appears that things improved with satellite and aerial photography. Did this kind of information make a difference and prevent another battlefield surprise like the one you just described?

Hamdani: First of all, yes, the intelligence information was excellent, and got better because of a number of factors. I felt that the Arab party that might have sent us information was either King Hussein [Jordan] or King Abdullah [Saudi Arabia], because one of them visited us then. But at the same time, there was coordination with the American military attaché in Baghdad. At the same time, we had aircraft with better cameras for photography. We also had good sources of strategic intelligence, such as from the spies inside Iran as well as other countries around the area. We also had good wireless eavesdropping. This was new equipment [for us], so the electronic war was going well. The most important thing [in limiting new surprises] was that the Iranians attacked the same area once again; they did not go to another sector. Therefore, we had the opportunity to watch them for a whole year and see how they progressed. So the enemy did not surprise us from another front, but came from the same place, and we knew exactly what to expect.

Murray: I noticed that in 1984–1985 your regiment, Hamza, was moving between the major frontline combat and then back to Baghdad to rest and reset. Was this the normal procedure for just the Republican Guard, or was there an effort made to do this with all the army formations to keep them refreshed from fighting?

Hamdani: Yes, this was only for the Republican Guard. Because it was a strategic force, all kinds of special operations units would come back. Once they accomplished their missions, all strategic reserves would come back in order to re-organize their structure, training, and supplies.

Discussion Seven

The 1986 Al-Fao Campaign and Baghdad's Misinterpretation of Iranian Strategy—Traitors in the Iraqi Leadership—Prisoners of War— Operation *Dawn*—Iraqi Casualty Competition and the "Bedouin Mentality"

Woods: In the Al-Fao campaign, you mention that the enemy took you by surprise. You noted earlier that in February of 1986, intelligence had improved. Nevertheless, here the Iranians were able to take the Iraqi command by surprise. You suggest that there was some sort of deception operation meant to distract the Iraqi high command, while the Iranians were seizing Al-Fao. Could you describe the circumstance of the initial Iranian offensive to seize Al-Fao, why you think they were successful, and if and where there were deception operations associated with it?

Hamdani: I remember this well because I participated in the area at the field level and saw the intelligence that was coming in from those doing the monitoring. They confirmed that the attack was going to be toward the VII Corps in the south. However, the Iranians deceived our strategic intelligence desk [in Baghdad] into believing that the attack would come against the III Corps [central] sector, which was the same sector [the Iranians] had attacked in 1984, 1985, and 1986.[57] The field knew the truth while the military strategists in Baghdad said, "No, the attack is going to happen here in the [central sector]." So there was a disagreement between the two levels, and the military strategists in Baghdad refused to accept the facts the commanders had seen on the ground.

Woods: What did the planners in Baghdad think was happening?

Hamdani: They believed that the Iranians would conduct operations in the same way that they had in 1984, 1985, and 1986—attacking the same sector of the VI Corps. The strategy had a flaw that was visible from the field—I saw personally that the enemy was going to attack the VII Corps, when I went on reconnaissance missions. We could see that the Iranians were dropping the boats they were going to use, building observation posts, and making gaps between the orchards to stockpile their war supplies. They were building logistic roads with their corps of engineers. So we could see that the Iranians were going to attack in this direction, but back in our headquarters they dismissed this as just a trick and believed that the main attack was going to come against the VI Corps.

Woods: Were the Iranians trying to run a deception indicating that they were going to repeat the previous years' attacks on the sector?

Hamdani: Well, there was interception of radio communications just inside the area of the VI Corps, because there were strategic wireless stations to indicate that there would be something there, but there was no ground activity. So the Iraqi strategic leadership sent a mass group of loyal Ba'ath party members [militia] to the VI Corps sector to cut down the reeds.

One person I remember playing a role in this was Wafiq Al-Samarra'i [director deputy military of intelligence responsible for the Iran branch].[58] It was possible he dealt with [these decisions] at that time, as he was in charge and so could have been the one behind the disagreement [with the forward forces]. He [Al-Samarra'i] is currently serving as the security advisor to Iraqi President Jalal Talabani.

For us, [Al-Samarra'i] is a traitor. Saddam trusted this man to the highest degree. He knew many secrets that many generals did not know. He was a smart person, but also selfish. He would not allow any good Iraqi intelligence officer to get promoted or to work his way up the chain of command. Even the director of Iraqi intelligence did not have much control over this man because of his close ties with Saddam. [For example], we started to exchange some POWs between Iraq and Iran, mostly injured, young soldiers, and so forth. One of these Iranian prisoners was a very high-value POW from the Iraqi perspective, to the point where Saddam met personally with this person a number of times. At one point, Wafiq Al-Samarra'i returned this most valuable person to Iran without Saddam's knowledge or that of the intelligence director. This was really dangerous. When the individual arrived back in Iran, we had at the time a spy at the Iranian operations headquarters in Tehran. And we also had a network of spies working for Iraqi intelligence [in Iran]. The second day this POW made it back to Iran, all these spies and our agent in the Iranian intelligence headquarters were executed.

Woods: Who was this POW? Was he a general or a senior spy?

Hamdani: No, he was a vague individual, but he had a lot of information from Iranian intelligence. We knew he worked with or was a member of the Iranian intelligence, but we were not so sure about what he did specifically. He was an ambiguous and important individual, with a dark cloud on top of him.

Woods: Do you remember his name?

Hamdani: No, I can't remember, by God. We had a general in the Iranian operations working on behalf of the Iraqi intelligence, and immediately after this

POW went back to Iran, this general and his cell that provided us with information were executed. This was in the same year [1986].

Once information about these actions of Wafiq Al-Samarra'i reached Saddam, he was so upset and frustrated that he dropped Al-Samarra'i from being second in command of Iraqi intelligence to being an intelligence officer for the VII Corps. I remember going on a reconnaissance mission in the VII Corps' area of operations, and I had to stop at the corps headquarters, because one of the commanders needed to talk to me. And when I came in, there was General Wafiq, and I will never forget how he was sitting. I asked him, "What are you doing here?" and he did not answer me. So when the corps commander came in I asked him what General Wafiq was doing there, he replied that General Wafiq had made a terrible mistake that would normally deserve execution by Iraqi standards, but because Saddam loved him and their close ties, he just dropped him down from his former position.

After he fled to Europe in 1992, we received further information.[59] Qusay, Saddam's son, asked me, "Can you believe that Wafiq Al-Samarra'i was a traitor since 1982? He worked for the Iranian service since 1982." I told Qusay that this was impossible. So he showed me a file about the general since that time, and it told about how Talabani recruited him in 1982 to work for both Talabani and the Iranian services. This was really a shock. This man was the reservoir of all the intelligence information that Saddam received.

Woods: So what was motivating Samarra'i, especially in 1982? Why do you think he betrayed his country?

Hamdani: It was so strange that we could not believe that he would do this. This is why, as I mentioned earlier, he [Al-Samarra'i] never allowed anybody smart or experienced to become an intelligence officer or to make it through the ranks. Every time someone would make his way, the general would find an excuse to get rid of him.

Murray: How was he able to work his way into Saddam's circle?

Hamdani: First of all, he was very smart. We had other smart people, like the chief of staff of the army, but to get close to President Saddam Hussein one had to possess the ability to read [Saddam's] mind and express his opinion. Al-Samarra'i would read the other generals in discussions and lay out the groundwork, such that it would sound like whatever decision Saddam had decreed, it was the right one. He would use his skills to manipulate situations, and in this way, he earned Saddam's trust. This needs to be understood in the context of Saddam's rarely giving much authority and trust to others. However, once that trust was gained, he would trust the person until proven otherwise. At present, the Anfal trial that is prosecuting the former minister of defense and the chief of staff of the army is nothing compared to the role of Wafiq Al-Samarra'i, who was in charge of the intelligence of the Anfal operation.[60]

Woods: In the specific incident regarding the release of the senior Iranian intelligence officer captured, how did General Al-Samarra'i explain this? I understand that he said it was a mistake, but was the idea that he was not intending to release him, or that he hoped to turn him into a double agent? How did he explain this to Saddam?

Hamdani: By God, I don't know the details, but he had an incredible skill to convince others and earn their trust. But from what I heard from others close to Saddam, he tried to convince Saddam that he tried to use to the prisoner as a double agent inside the headquarters back in Tehran. Al-Samarra'i managed to convince Saddam that they should use the prisoner as a double agent, but Saddam was upset that Al-Samarra'i did not go back to him to get the final decision on whether to release him.

Woods: Getting back to the 1986 Al-Fao campaign. Can you describe for us the specific conditions faced by the VII Corps and the initial Iranian attack? Why do you think the Iranians were successful as quickly as they were, and what events precipitated the panic and breakdown within the Iraqi forces?

Hamdani: First of all, the Iranians were able to work freely [without Iraqi interference] and mobilize their troops and reserves in the VII Corps area of operations. Our strategic observation posts focused on the VI Corps, and so they observed little. Second, the Iranians were [militarily] superior in the Al-Fao area. Iraq had only the 26th Division for defense in the area. The force that attacked was as big as an Iranian corps, along with an intense artillery bombardment and thousands of quick boat crossings. It was a short distance from the orchard lines to Iraqi positions that provided the necessary protection and cover [to the Iranians]. At night, right before dawn, waves of Iranians suddenly attacked.

We had our defenses along the river. In these areas there was nothing but orchards. There are three main roads into Al-Fao from the northwest. The first road runs alongside the Euphrates River to the Shatt al-Arab, the second runs up to Basra, and the third come in from Um-Qasr in the west.

Iraqi commanders had established and built up their defenses sufficient to deter a secondary attack, but not a major one. That is, it was sufficient enough in case of a deception attack. Most of the focus of the defensive line was back in the area of the VI Corps. Even the VII Corps commander was subordinated to the VI Corps commander. At that time we were astonished at this stupidity; we couldn't believe our leadership was this stupid.

The enemy attacked Al-Kharnoubiyah area in this direction at the same time as in the area of Um Al-Sababikh Island. These attacks were at the brigade level, although there was a division that crossed the Um Al-Ma'aber area. There was meticulous [Iranian] preparation for this battle; I witnessed a lot of it.

Murray: Was there any particular Iranian general or Iranian group of officers who had come up with this plan? Who do you think was responsible?

Hamdani: [The mission was planned by] the chief of staff of the Iranian army and the minister of defense who adopted this effort at the highest level. It was called "Fajr operation," or Operation *Dawn*. The commanders were from the new Iranian leadership, representing a mix of the army, the Pasdaran, and others, along with some officers from the naval forces.

Woods: This turns out to have been some of the most complex conventional combat of the war. The Iranians seem to have integrated their ground forces, used multiple point crossings, integrated airpower, and coordinated considerable artillery. It was also a joint combined arms operation since it included Iranian naval forces operating simultaneously with air and ground forces. Can you provide us any additional insights?

Hamdani: Yes, [the Iranians] demonstrated a high-quality performance of integrated operations. There were thousands of boats that fit 400 people, rushing in before dawn. These were rubber boats, wooden boats, and big boats all transporting thousands of soldiers in a few moments under the cover of intense artillery and air bombardment of the area. We downed some of the Iranian aircraft and the recovered pilots gave us information about the attacks. These were important since our leaders would not believe our reports without that evidence. One of the POWs was an air force captain, and he gave us the plan about how they had [crossed to the Fao Peninsula] and told us that there was at least a corps level force in the attack. This was when the strategic command back in headquarters [Baghdad] finally began to pay attention. To confirm that he knew what he was talking about, the captain also mentioned that the Iranians probably had more than 1,000 Iraqi POWs back at their headquarters. But even with this report and headquarters acknowledging that this was part of the main attack, Baghdad still had worries about a secondary attack back in the [central] VI Corps sector.

Woods: Did the Iranians use any form of naval infantry or marines for landings along the coast during this operation?

Hamdani: No. One cannot do landings along these coasts because of their limited depth. Even our navy did not operate in this area, and our navy was the one with the capabilities to do so. [The coastal area to the south of the main attack], approximately 3 kilometers from us, was not suitable for boat landings because the deep water is too far from the shore. As for the role of the Iranian navy, they shelled this area and helped in other landings and transportation operations along the Al-Fao Peninsula.

Everything was happening so quickly that even after the battle started, the leadership in Baghdad and Basra still believed there was another main attack coming [to the north]. After these long battles, we went back to the first supply channel.

Each one of our echelons had a command, the Shatt al-Arab command, the strategic command, and the Um-Qasr command. Moreover, tactical commands among fighting units were organized in a complicated way. In order for us to gather forces and attack the enemy in a certain location, it took more than 3 to 4 hours to coordinate the maneuver out of the area. This problem resulted from the huge re-deployment of Iraqi troops and all the traffic.

The nature of the terrain in this area was so dusty in dry periods and muddy when raining, that it was always difficult to maneuver. We could only stay on the roads, and with all the traffic funneled along the only two roads, it was terrible—the infantry, the BMPs, the armor. Because of the fact that there were only two roads, the Iranian forces were able continuously to shell both. They knew about the terrain conditions and that the roads were the only way in or out for transportation. The enemy was just on the other side [of the Shatt], and so they were able to see us. The front was narrow, and the emergency medical evacuation service never had sufficient time to catch up with the soldiers. As a result, there were many losses caused by the intense shelling. Most of the palm trees and orchards were destroyed by the bombardment that occurred. The land became barren. I had never seen such intense bombing throughout the war. It was a very, very difficult battle and extremely intense, especially along the line.

Woods: Given what you have just described, what would a military force need to operate in an area like Al-Fao? Taking into account this unique terrain, even within the Middle East, what is required to be successful militarily in this environment?

Hamdani: The answer to this question points to a weakness in the Iraqi strategic thinking. It was Bedouin and not professional. I was resentful of the Iraqi strategic approach at the time, thinking it was wrong. However, this [Al-Fao] was Iraqi territory taken by the Iranians, so I was determined to retake it. We considered this attack as a stab at the dignity of the Iraqi leadership. This proves that this is Bedouin and not strategic thinking.

In 1994, I discussed this issue in a personal meeting I had with Saddam Hussein, where we exchanged opinions. He had sent for me when I objected to the proposal to reoccupy Kuwait in 1994. So the main discussion led to discussions of other battles, including this one. During 1986 and 1987, my recommendations were that as long as the enemy achieved superiority in troops in an area that neutralized our armor and air force, the Republican Guard armored troops and any Army armored divisions should leave and let the infantry take over. The armored units should go in the direction of Muhammarah [Khorramshahr] and Al-Ahwaz, because it was a good area to operate armor and block those cities. This would have given balance to our strategic position, and we could strike all the maintenance and logistics lines that were coming from the enemy's side to support the Fao operation. This [maneuver] would have weakened the Iranian support farther south. Saddam

Hussein said to me, "You always object. Why are you objecting?" and I said to him, "Sir, our strategic problem is that you used our armor for an infantry operation—the same mistake the British made in World War I."

Murray: Was this the problem with the Iraqi army's doctrine, or did Saddam play a role in this?

Hamdani: It was a combination of the two. Part of it was a mentality among the high-ranking general officers, but it also stemmed from Saddam Hussein's insistence on recapturing Al-Fao. It was in part Saddam's ignorance about how to use armor, but it was also a flaw that we had in our understanding about how to use armor. We knew the mentality of the British, and we were supposed to benefit from the experience of the Germans and the Americans, when they used armored forces in World War II. As young men following the history of World War II, we much admired the ideas of [Heinz] Guderian and [Erwin] Rommel, as well as those of [George] Patton.[61] The way to learn is to read history. Saddam Hussein did not, nor did many of our generals. Not surprisingly, they did not know how to use armor; most of them believed that armor just supported the infantry.

Woods: Besides yourself, who were the other maneuverists and people who understood the concept of armored maneuver?

Hamdani: Surely there were quite a few other generals who had the same opinions as I. But because of the environment, they were afraid of expressing their opinions. But we had [the same] problems as other Third World leaders.

We had the problem of inflexibility of usage with the armored forces; we always favored tying the infantry to tank divisions. This is the nature of the Third World generals; they are not creative when it comes to maneuvering. For us, the Israeli generals were the professors, since they adopted the German method in using armored forces. The Eastern mentality, when it comes to armor maneuvering, is limited. What Winston Churchill said is true and wonderful: "You win the wars by maneuvering and fighting. And the great general is the one whose maneuvers exceed his battles."[62] That is something we lack in Arab military forces. Since their way of thinking is more Western, the Israelis resorted to more maneuvering than fighting. We, the Easterners, even the Russians, prefer fighting to maneuvering.

Murray: It strikes me that at least early in the war, Saddam clearly regarded the number of casualties suffered by Iraqi forces as an indication of military effectiveness, much like World War I generals. To Saddam, a successful battle had a large number of casualties as opposed to the way I think that many maneuverists, and certainly we Americans, think successful battle has few casualties.

Hamdani: This is true. Our commanders would even brag to one another about how many men they lost, saying, "I lost this number of soldiers!"

What we need to understand is the way our [Iraqi-Eastern] mentality is and how it dominates the thinking processes. An Eastern way and a Western way, an educated way and the other one less educated, all this plays a role in wars. For instance, since Saddam Hussein was a Bedouin and came from a small village, he had the tendency to emphasize battles and killing. Saddam said to me, "I don't know why you always try to take the heart out of it. You think too much before you execute any plan." He was always ready to go straight toward an objective a great distance away. However, in the history of war, we understand that the more you maneuver, the more you can confuse the enemy. The more you confuse the enemy, the fewer losses you will have and the greater casualties you inflict on him. Take the example of Napoleon Bonaparte's occupation of Vienna in 1805, where he seized the Austrian capital without a fight.

Discussion Eight

Republican Guard Expansion and the Response to Al-Fao—Hussein Kamel—General Hamdani's Command Obstacles—1987 Iranian Attack on Basra and Casualty Inflation—Shalamjah: The Somme of the Iran-Iraq War—Hamdani's Venture through the Front and the Battlefield Conditions

Woods: General, in your memoirs, you mention that in May of 1986, immediately after the battle for Fao, the Republican Guard was expanded. Can you talk about how this was accomplished and what qualitative challenges you confronted in expanding the force? What were your perceptions of the quality of the Republican Guard after the expansion was complete?

Hamdani: Saddam Hussein considered Fao as a major challenge, since he was always interested in liberating Iraqi territory taken by Iran. There was also an Iranian challenge. I remember hearing at the time Ali Khamenei saying, "If Saddam Hussein liberates or gets back Fao, I would be more than happy to go to Baghdad and congratulate him on taking back the territory."[63] This is the type of challenge that Saddam Hussein jumped at. He realized that the troops he could rely on [to retake Fao] were the Republican Guard, if he could provide them a chance to train and expand on a larger scale.

So Saddam came up with the decision to double the force of the Republican Guard to bring it to the size of 8 to 10 divisions. He immediately set in motion a major program and opened a Republican Guard enlistment system with excellent financial incentives. There was always a selective process for joining the Republican Guard, but this time the recruitment was open to the public. We recruited at universities for students who possessed a decent level of education and also involved tribal leaders to recruit from the tribes.

The army established a large camp in the area of Al-Habbaniyah, in Al-Anbar, to receive these large numbers of volunteers. At the same time, it continued the selective process of picking qualified officers from the Iraqi army as command-ing officers. For approximately 6 to 8 months, the system worked and was able to form several [new] armor and infantry formations at the base. These were the 7th Republican Guard brigade, the 8th Republican Guard armored infantry brigade, the 9th Republican Guard armored brigade, and the 12th Commando brigade. This last group was not so much commandos as they were a force somewhat in between spe-cial forces and infantry, like the [American] Rangers. We called them Maghaweer. There were also the 21st Maghaweer brigade, the 26th Special Forces brigade, the 16th Special Forces brigade, and the 26th Naval Special Forces brigade, the sea mis-sion brigade, the frogmen. This group trained at Al-Habbaniyah Lake on diving and attacking [from an amphibious environment]. They brought in experts, who I think were Egyptians, to train [our soldiers] in these operations, as well as some of the senior officers who worked for the navy's special forces and understood the underwater technologies.

The army also expanded the artillery forces with other battalions. It started the Republican Guard's armament development and supply process, as well as the Republican Guard's extensive training in restricted area operations, such as in orchards and soft-soil areas. The Republican Guard's Al-Madina Al-Munawara, Hammurabi, and Baghdad divisions were all created. Al-Madina and Hammurabi were armored divisions, while Nebuchadnezzar and Baghdad [divisions] were both infantry. And then there was the commando division within the Special Forces. However, Saddam was unable to form 8 to 10 divisions. In addition, the army was able to form and add to the five divisions that already existed within the Republican Guard. They added the 1st, 2d, and 10th brigades, and the 4th Special Forces brigade. They were all a part of the Republican Guard, which was organized into a corps of five divisions.

There was an extensive training curriculum, day and night, and we reached a limited level of preparation. Saddam Hussein continuously followed up with us to see how our training was coming, and the readiness of our forces. Hus-sein Kamel was the Republican Guard's supervisor and was in charge of reviewing any requests we submitted.[64] Anything that we asked for, he provided. He was also the main point of contact between Saddam and us. There were large amounts of money spent on the budget for the recruiting and training programs. Any officer nominated (to join the Republican Guard) had to report for duty at the training center within 72 hours; otherwise, his brigade or division commander would be punished. We had several active firing ranges and training grounds that would run 24 hours a day.

Woods: Did you put all the recruits together? Were the experienced mem-bers of the Republican Guard mixed in with the new recruits, or were they divided by division, or what?

Hamdani: This was an elective process. I would elect candidates and sign the roster, meaning that I would be responsible for who was selected. Then I would give the roster to Hussein Kamel, where an order from the Presidency Council would be issued immediately to the Ministry of Defense for the individual officer to report.

Murray: How did you ensure that the volunteers the Republican Guard was getting were of the highest quality?

Hamdani: The commander would pick them himself.

Woods: What kind of general was Hussein Kamel? What was your opinion of him in the 1986 timeframe? Was he more of a soldier or a bureaucrat?

Hamdani: Hussein Kamel was an executive agent who would honor our needs and had the same authority as the president [with respect to moving issues through the bureaucracy]. The minute we would submit a request, he would not even question or ask why. He was Saddam's office director. For example, if we were to request a boat for an armored division, it would not be an issue, because Kamel did not know anything about this sort of thing. He was not a professional; he was an instrument to enforce authority. It was up to me to be accurate and intelligent about requests, because even if I were to ask for an aircraft, he would provide it. Hussein Kamel was a part of this long chain of formation committees. It was something of a bureaucracy when it came to requests, but because of his authority under Saddam, he could shortcut the processes to get everything done as quickly as possible.

Woods: When you transferred to the Madina Al-Munawara Division as the first adjutant to the director[65] in September of 1986, you made a comment in your memoir: "This was followed by the formation of the Hammurabi command out of the 17th Republican Guard Armored brigade, which faced difficult conditions since the Al-Fao battle that cannot be mentioned here." What were these difficult conditions?

Hamdani: Yes, there were difficulties with the division commander, whose name was Brigadier General Ahmad Hammash Al-Tikriti. He was courageous, but plainly stupid and possessed only a limited education. I had many clashes with him over division preparation plans, and so it was hard for me to build the division, because he always had objections to my recommendations and the decisions I made. I often stayed up until the morning reviewing decisions (we did not have computers; everything was done by hand). I would lay out certain plans that I had spent all night putting together, and then he would disregard them altogether. These difficulties were a terrible obstacle, and I could not cross him, since he was my direct commander. It is hard for anyone to work under the command of a stupid leader of limited education, not knowing how to cross him and needing to comply with orders, but at the same time wanting to do the right thing.

Woods: Can you describe the fourth Iranian attack on Basra, in the period of early 1987? Did anything change from the previous attack, or is this another case of more of the same from the Iranians?

Hamdani: It was a small theater of operations, even the main battlefield. The focus was on an Iranian move before the main attack. It was an attempt to deceive our forces on the ground. The Iranian attack failed terribly, and there was a competition between the [Iraqi] III and VII Corps commanders over who defeated the enemy. Both commanders were uneducated and primitive, one was a friend of President Saddam and a major Ba'athist; the other a friend of General Al-Duri. Their names were Tali' Al-Duri, for the III Corps, and General Maher 'Abd Rashid, for the VII Corps. Saddam made his son marry Maher's daughter. Qusay married Maher's daughter in order to honor a promise [the commander of the VII Corps promised success in liberating Al-Fao, and gave his daughter to show his certainty], which is an Arab tradition. Saddam was close to General Maher but had a disagreement with him later on. Saddam asked for his help in 1991 to suppress the uprisings.

Back to this one-day attack, it caused a bigger problem in Iran than Iraq. In order for the III Corps commander to prove that he defeated the Iranian attack, he gave some figures for the Iranian losses—a large number that was completely unrealistic. General Maher 'Abd Rashid knew he needed to be Saddam Hussein's favorite, and so he gave an even larger number. There was competition between the commanders that was almost funny. The III Corps commander came back and said, "We made sure that we doubled the losses of the enemy." What happened is that Saddam Hussein felt satisfied because of the large losses for the Iranian army following Al-Fao. To make matters worse, the Iranians then came back with propaganda saying that it was "the attack of the million." So to the strategic leadership back in Baghdad, the corps commanders repeated that they caused all this damage in the sectors of the 6th and 3d Divisions. Such losses would obviously affect the capability of the Iranian forces all along the border, so everybody relaxed.

Woods: So in other words, they inflated the numbers because of personal competition, and this resulted in a false estimate for the entire front.

Hamdani: That is correct. [Commanders] started giving leave, which was not allowed before this, because they were always waiting at the front line for the Iranian forces. But when these reports came out that the damage [to Iran] was doubled, everyone relaxed. The readiness of the forces went back to the normal level.

Woods: When did it become known that the estimates of the III and the VII Corps commanders were double that of what the Iranian losses actually were?

Hamdani: Well, the peace of mind that the enemy suffered such big losses led people to think that Iran would need at least 6 months to plan for a major attack. In the meantime, after just 2 weeks, the enemy staged an extremely sudden attack.

They entered via Al-Muhammarah [Khorramshahr] area, via Bubyan, the Fish Lake area, and Al-Ghuzayal areas, and advanced until they reached Basra's bridges.

Murray: This was across areas that had excellent fortifications and fields of fire. This area was well known to the Iraqis—it was an area that had been fought over for a consistent period. So while there was surprise, everybody knew what the territory was and what the ground was where the battles were taking place—correct?

Hamdani: Here is where the lie of both commanders became known, and Baghdad finally understood that the generals had inflated the numbers 10 times over what their corps had actually destroyed. In fact, the entire losses were not even equal to one of the Iranian corps.

At this time the Iranians also launched a battle in the sector of Shalamjah along the border. The Iranian troops went in; we had held the same positions; and they did not utilize any maneuvering, but just fought face-to-face. This type of combat continued for many days. It was very difficult. More than 5,000 cannon and tank muzzles gathered in this small area, firing at each other. The way this area was bombed was unbelievable: [the result was] massive destruction.

Woods: This is the area that everybody sees in the documentaries that looks just like the Western Front from 1917–1918, with the terrain completely transformed by the artillery.

Hamdani: I personally called it "the Somme of the Iran-Iraq War."

Murray: It seems that the Iranians are still showing a complete lack of imagination and flexibility. That is, and the Somme analogy is particularly interesting in this way, that the Iranians were simply repeating, and repeating, and repeating, believing that the losses they were inflicting on the other side were going to cause the Iraqis to soon, tomorrow or the next day, collapse.

Hamdani: This area reached a level where some of the corps there lost communication since the Iranians attacked in such massive human waves. The minister of defense, Adnan Khairallah, came and I met with him in this place called Jbatsi.[66] From farther north, we were able to get a better view of the battlefield. General Khairallah then assigned the Republican Guard a mission with unrealistic timing, one impossible to accomplish in the timeframe. That is when the disasters happened. Some of the brigades [were destroyed] and many troops were killed. The situation worsened to the point where my commander Ahmad Hammash could not use the phone to talk with higher headquarters and get support. No one was able to reach a phone or even a communication station because of the extensive bombing and the Iranian presence. You could not see a 10-meter area that had not been bombed.

There were two defense lines. One was called the Jasser line, while the other was called Al-Da'ich. They both fell under the control of Iranian forces. At this point, the commander was asked to report on the status of our troops. My commander [Major General Ahmad Hammash] gave me a look, as if asking me what to do. There was constant infiltration by the Iranian forces; they infiltrated 200 meters here and 500 meters there, such that it was difficult for us even to maneuver our forces on our side of the lines.

Headquarters in Baghdad [placed] huge pressure on Commander Ahmad Hammash and the III Corps commander. There was no communication available with our units. Therefore, I understood that the way he had looked at me was a call for help. I told him that I would go and check what the status was. I left knowing that I might not be able to go any farther than 300, 200, or even 50 meters. I got in my jeep and left. I went for about 50 meters, where the bombing [and bomb damage] was so intense that no regular vehicle could pass. The battlefield was very small, so it always seemed as though you were at the front. The bombing and artillery were continuous.

Woods: Did the staff in Baghdad during this time, or even the corps staffs, really understand the conditions on the field, what it looked like for those brigades that were in the defense? Did they appreciate how small the battlefield was, and physically, how difficult it would be to move or to resupply?

Hamdani: The headquarters in Baghdad definitely asked us to advance a greater distance. They wanted us to push the enemy back to the border and provide them with better reporting. Down on the ground, those at the front line were not able to report, because the Iranian units were actually inside the perimeters of corps and division headquarters. The expectations of those up at headquarters were completely disconnected from what was occurring on the ground.

At one point, an armored personnel carrier arrived at our headquarters. I went to the driver, who was a captain in one of the companies. They were desperate [terrified and disoriented]. I told them to keep moving to the front. He just looked at me without answering. So I joined him and again told them to move and they did until we reached Al-Da'ich, the first line. Nothing but massacred tanks and dead people surrounded the area—tens of dead people every 100 meters, tens of tanks burning. The situation I saw was the same as I had only seen in the movies. Then I reached a place where I found a barrier of three Iranian Russian tanks, two T–55s and one T–62. I got out and started looking for the division headquarters, which was isolated in one place, somewhere under the ground. This is where the V Corps headquarters was located. There were tens of soldiers on the areas above ground, most injured and bleeding. You could see their blood dripping through the stairs in the structure. So I went down into the headquarters. [Inside] there were the staffs of the V Corps all huddled together. I wrote this story in detail in my memoir. When I got down there I wanted to get the injured out, to get the most gravely injured out, like the ones whose guts were out rather than the ones hit by shrapnel.

The 5 kilometers that I visited took from 9:00 in the morning till 6:30 in the evening for a round trip, as an example of how difficult the situation was. So I knew what the situation really was. As far as taking the injured on the armored personnel carrier, as soon as we entered open territory, we were hit by Iranian fire, and most of the injured became martyrs. The whole idea in recounting my experience is to give you a picture of this situation that is probably reflective of the Battle of Somme in World War I, but one that happened in the Iran-Iraq War. We should have had the armored corps maneuver around rather than strike directly at this area.

Discussion Nine

July 1987 Republican Guard Command Changes—Battlefield Missiles—Halabjah—Factors of Post-1987 Shift in "Correlation of Forces" toward Iraq—Planning Effort for Al-Fao Offensive—Use of Helicopters—Front of 1988—July 1988 Iraqi Incursion through to Ahvaz and the Mujahideen-e-Khalq

Woods: General, you mention in your memoir that on 25 July 1987, after the Al-Fao campaign, "Many changes occurred in the formation of the upper echelons of our command; among the changes the replacement of the Republican Guard commander by the director of military operations, [a man] known for his courage and achievements." What happened that required the removal of the Republican Guard commander?

Hamdani: There were a few reasons for this. The first reason was that Saddam Hussein realized that this was the last chance to achieve victory in the war, and therefore, he needed an experienced and competent commander to achieve his goals. These were the qualities of [the new commander] General Ayad Al-Rawi. This man was courageous and persistent in achieving his goals, even though he possessed only limited strategic military education. So he was promoted to the head of the Republican Guard.

Woods: Was he considered a professional, tactical commander, but lacking in experience at the senior command level? What was lacking in his "strategic education"?

Hamdani: Well, this was a problem we had in the Iraqi army. The number of people with strategic education was small. But he was a professional soldier and disciplined. He was also meticulous with details. At the same time, he was not a Tikriti from Saddam Hussein's family like so many of the Republican Guard commanders were. Thus, there would not be any flattery from the rest of the command; it would all be on a professional level. He was the kind of commander who, if you [were told] to execute a plan, you'd [better] do it the right way, because he would not cut [you] any slack.

Woods: The way you describe this, it seems like it may have been one of the best decisions Saddam made during the war.

Hamdani: Yes. And he chose the right person for the position. What is important is that he was not the flattering type. He was an original soldier who was not afraid to say what is right is right and what is wrong is wrong. If he did not agree with you, he would express his opinions without fear.[67]

Woods: As I look at the history of the Iraqi military—back to 1980 and all the way through the end of the campaign in 2003—Iraq probably has more experience with battlefield missiles, such as the Scud, Luna or Ra'd [RAAD],[68] and Astros than almost any other nation. Can you tell me something about battlefield missiles from the point of view of a field commander? Did the division commanders get involved with the targeting of longer range missiles?

Hamdani: Regarding the Scud missiles, there was no influence on the field—strategic command had the only decision. They were the ones in charge of making the decision for targeting. On the division level, the ground division and brigade commanders had no involvement in the decisionmaking processes [regarding missile targeting]. As far as the Luna and Ra'd missiles, Ra'd is made in Iraq, and other than that is no different than the Luna. These were used at the corps level—the targets were chosen at this level. For [ground] Ra'd missiles, they were under the command of the divisions.

Woods: Moving ahead to March of 1988—could you describe for us what the events surrounding the Iraqi 34th Division in and around Halabjah, between 13 and 15 March of 1988? These events precipitated a well-known use of WMD but I want to better understand what happened to that division tactically.

Hamdani: The Iranians were quite superior in the area of Halabjah due to the great cooperation of the Kurds there, not to mention that the mountainous terrain is well suited for infiltration operations between the valleys. The 34th Division was unable to overcome the infiltration ground offensive by the Iranians. Moreover, at this point the division commander was captured. Unfortunately, we refer to this division as the "unlucky division," especially as the division commander was also killed in 1992 by the Kurds. I believe they were doing a joint operation. This was the same division, but obviously a different commander. The commander [captured] in 1988 was not released. So no matter what this division did, it never had the luck needed to succeed.

Woods: Wasn't the 34th Division also the division that came down to relieve your Baghdad division in al-Kut in 2003?[69]

Hamdani: Yes, that was it.

Woods: It seems their luck did not improve—as they were surrounded by U.S. Marines and destroyed in 2003.

Hamdani: Yes, but the 34th Division commander was not killed in the 2003 war. However, they killed him in the aftermath of the war, because he was a Shia and a member of the Republican Guard. The Iranians killed him in approximately January of 2004. Even earlier, another one of the division's commanders conspired against the division, and he was turned over to an investigation council and incarcerated for 7 years.

Woods: In April 1988, after almost 2 years of Iranian occupation, Iraq managed to recapture the Al-Fao Peninsula. You have described how Saddam personally spent much time planning the operation. You also wrote that the entire planning effort occurred in secret. Even the Iraqi army chief of staff and the head of the general staff were never informed of the planning in order to enhance the quantity of the deception. Could you explain the planning that went into the Al-Fao operation, and more specifically, explain the deception that was run against Iran—and to some extent Iraq's own senior military staff?

Hamdani: Yes, this [deception story] is true. The reason for it was that Saddam Hussein realized that he had no better opportunity to reoccupy this area and compensate for the losses that had already occurred. There was an agreement to enforce the Security Council's Resolution 598, issued in 1987, and the Iranians had just launched major attacks and had large forces in northern Iraq, including Halabjah. The entire northern area was occupied by Iran, in addition to the southern sector of Al-Fao and a part of the eastern border. So Saddam was running out of time. This was his last chance to rectify these losses that had happened along the borders.

Murray: One of the fascinating things about this is that somehow between 1987 and the launching of the Al-Fao offensive, there was clearly a major change in what the Soviets called "correlation of forces."[70] The balance favored the Iranians, with their small gains. Then, suddenly, the balance shifts in favor of the Iraqis. Did the Iranians finally exhaust themselves with their constant murderous battles? Or was that the degree of professionalization of the Iraqi army and Republican Guard had finally reached a point where they could win a major victory?

Hamdani: All of this is true. It was both a matter of the increased training and experience of the Republican Guards, as well as the decrease of the Iranians due to the large number of battles they conducted and the losses they had suffered. This last point especially affected the quality of their forces.

Most importantly, though, is that the charm of the revolution and the charisma of their leader, Ayatollah Khomeini, languished. The losses and the amount of destruction inflicted on the Iranian economy by the war of the tankers were a factor, and in addition, Iraq had destroyed much of their economy. So the charm of the revolution, as each revolution and each new movement has its power, the power and the holiness of Khomeini significantly declined. Moreover, the willingness of Iranian soldiers to sacrifice themselves weakened considerably.

Despite the experiences and expertise gained, the spirit always weakens in the long wars. Take Alexander the Great's army, for example. Due to the continuous wars he undertook, its morale weakened to the point where Alexander's soldiers started to cry like babies.

Woods: We would like to know more about the planning effort for the Al-Fao campaign and the relationship between the planning and deception. You noted that for this operation you had a small planning staff. This sounds a lot like Saddam's planning method for the invasion of Kuwait in 1990, where there was a very small team that stayed in contact with Saddam and planned the mission with a significant number of senior staff officers left out of the loop. So what was the key to the deception? How were they able to trick both the Iranians and the senior Iraqi military?

Hamdani: Saddam Hussein was able to accomplish the planning for the Republican Guard Corps and the VII Regular Army corps in a smart way with the support of the deputy chief of staff of the army for operations, General Hussein Rashid. He was the commander of the Republican Guard before General Ayad Al-Rawi. General Al-Khazraji, the chief of staff of the army, knew about the general planning and that it was occurring, but he did not know exactly when it was going to happen or details about it.

My role in the planning of the operation was to take the latest version of the plans and go by plane to the Military Intelligence Directorate.[71] I used to pass by the backside of the building and meet with General Wafiq Al-Samarra'i, whom we discussed earlier as being on the Iranian payroll. [Interestingly], he was later reinstated to the same post as before [director of the general military intelligence directorate], following the Al-Fao loss. So I would go and see him without the knowledge of the intelligence officers, because I would use the back elevator, and then I would show him the plans we made at the Republican Guard headquarters.

There were only six of us who knew about the plan. General Wafiq Al-Samarra'i used to approach us regarding the safety of planning and the enemy intelligence. He wanted to get a feel if the Iranians were starting to suspect Iraqi preparations to liberate Al-Fao. Once I got these recommendations and other ideas, I would take them and go back to Baghdad Palace, the command headquarters for Saddam. I would go there to talk with General Hussein Rashid, the assistant of the chief of staff. I would hand the plan over to him and he would explain the points to Saddam. If Saddam had any questions, or anything requiring clarification, he would call me in. If he would make any recommendations or additions to the plan, I would take it back to the director of intelligence, meet with the deputy director of Iraqi intelligence, and then from there, fly back to Basra. So there was a circle.

Woods: Looking back, do you suspect that General Al-Samarra'i was passing this information to an Iranian contact?

Hamdani: I truly do not know. From an early stage, I did not suspect anything. But we realized later on that Wafiq Al-Samarra'i was passing much information to the Iranians according to certain instructions. He was not the one making the decisions, since there seems to have been someone more senior than Wafiq who would decide on what to pass to the Iranians. This was our conclusion.

The only good and comfortable thing in this tiresome job was the ST–10 American helicopter, with two fins, since it flew at a high level, unlike the Russian ones, which were troublesome to travel in. Moreover, the ST was more comfortable than the Russian one.[72] This was for the higher headquarters and was designated for traveling from Basra to Baghdad. That was the only time we could actually relax, as opposed to when we used Russian helicopters.

Murray: In your memoirs, you describe a battle just after Al-Fao, the battle for Shalamjah. Apparently, there was a lot of confusion in the planning because of last-minute changes to the designated hour of attack. Were these changes based on interference from the top? Despite the confusion, the operation was a success, but it strikes me that there must have been something going on at the senior level to drive all of this. Can you tell us about this?

Hamdani: We received intelligence that the Iranians were actually aware of the time of the attack, so they had to change it in order to keep the factor of surprise.

Murray: Was this the result of an Iranian spy in Iraqi headquarters or some other source?

Hamdani: We think that the wireless equipment was giving off signals that informed their command and the regional commands that the Iraqis were going to launch an attack the next day. It might have been spies, or a mistake that was intercepted from the wireless equipment. I am not sure.

Woods: Going back to the end of the Al-Fao campaign for a moment, you made it explicitly clear that Saddam ordered the defeated Iranians to be allowed to cross the back into Iran across the Shatt. You said the purpose was so that they could spread their sense of fear, defeat, and poor morale among the units stationed on the Iranian side. This was in line with Sun Tzu's idea of providing one's enemy with a "golden bridge." Provide the enemy with a way out and he won't fight as hard, using his retreat to your advantage. Did Saddam make this decision on the fly, or had he always planned to push Iran out of Al-Fao to let them spread the sense of defeat? Surely, this wasn't done for humanitarian reasons?

Hamdani: I was present at the time, actually. The reports started to come in, and we had not expected to liberate Al-Fao this [quickly]. The Iranians were starting to drop and fall apart and were fleeing across the bridge back to their side. So Saddam asked, among all the commanding generals who were there [such as] an Iraqi air force general, "What do you recommend? What is your opinion about how we can handle the situation? Is it better to strike the bridge now or later?" Then there was this suggestion to let them leave because of the psychological impact it would have. With low morale within the ranks of the Iranian forces, it would be hard for them to fight again. Saddam was just asking for recommendations on this hard-to-handle situation.

Woods: Moving to a more doctrinal issue, it seems that during the late 1980s there was an increasing use by the Iraqi army of helicopters in what the U.S. Army calls "air assault" operations. At one point you mention that over 100 helicopters airlifted Iraqi troops into the Kurdish areas. Yet one of the biggest disasters you described in your memoirs was the Iraqi helicopter assaults during the 2 August 1990 invasion of Kuwait.[73] What changed? Was the fact that the 1990 operation was at night or over unfamiliar terrain? What changed?

Hamdani: There were two factors. The lack of planning and preparation affected the operation against Kuwait because everything happened within 10 hours before the execution. They [the Iraqi army pilots] literally got the order 10 hours before the invasion of Kuwait. They lost 2 more hours looking for the helicopter commander. Then, because of their lack of planning, they were unfamiliar with the terrain, and that combined with the darkness and the hundreds of telephone poles in the area resulted in the disaster. They were not prepared for this.

Woods: This is quite a contrast to the successful use of helicopters by the Iraqi infantry in June of 1988, in and around the Majnun Islands. You mentioned in your memoirs that there was an "airdrop" of a regiment behind enemy lines during this operation.

Hamdani: Yes, this was the 16th and the 3d brigades of the special forces.

Woods: Can you give us a description of what was happening along the rest of the front during 1988? You have described the events in Al-Fao, but what was Iran's situation going into the summer of 1988?

Hamdani: As a matter of fact, the main Iranian forces were actually located up north, because of strategic targeting. On the Iraqi side, we had most of our units, and the Republican Guard, centered in the south. So the manpower had really fallen in the south on the Iranian side in the 2 years leading up to the liberation of Al-Fao. Their center of gravity was now in the north. Because of the speed and method with which the Iraqi army retook Al-Fao, it did not allow much time for the main Iranian forces to reposition themselves to the south. This showed that the strategy to attack Al-Fao was the right solution.

The deception plan [in support of the Al-Fao attack] developed by the Iraqi leadership and approved by the chief of staff of the army consisted of a counterattack on the northern sector. We opened a decoy headquarters, employed numerous wireless stations, and [executed] large preparations. The 10th Armored Division deployed [to the north] as well as a Republican Guard headquarters. The purpose of all of this was to deceive the Iranians and make them believe that the next attack and [the bulk of] the Republican Guard would be moving to the north.

When thinking about strategic planning throughout the history of the Iraqi army, this might be the perfect example. We followed every single thing that we had studied and learned at the military academy and staff academy for strategic planning. After that, more than two corps moved south. [Remember] we went through five big battles in two months. This was a major strategic move. Moving the two corps was not easy. This was the highest point of experience and expertise that the Iraqi army reached.

All the while, the army was completing these missions in hot weather with temperatures anywhere from 58–60°C (about 140°F). The tank engines used to glow from the heat. Normally we would see smoke coming off the engine, but sometimes, in these conditions, we would actually see fire from the back of the vehicles. [This operation] was a nice finale and good compensation for our heavy losses and failures and the many mistakes we had made in the 8 years of the conflict.

Woods: You mention in your memoirs that when Saddam issued the order on 25 July 1988, to liberate every inch of Iraqi land, the III Corps actually went too far, all the way to Ahvaz. You said it waged an "unreasonable battle" with the Iranians at a placed called the Hamid military camp. Can you explain what this was all about?

Hamdani: Yes, the III Corps went beyond its [planned] limits. This was the Iranian second line of defense. They went for targets beyond what was planned. They wanted to go deeper into Iran to do more than just recapture Iraqi land, but to occupy some Iranian land. Really, this was the III Corps commander who was at fault. He recaptured the area that was assigned to him for the mission, but since the Iranian forces backed away and fell apart, he thought he would seize the opportunity to advance into Iran. The III Corps commander's name was General Salah Abboud, and he was actually one of the most qualified officers in the Iraqi army. He was the same III Corps commander during the [invasion and defense of] Kuwait. And he was the same one in Najaf during the last war, in 2003, as the senior military advisor to Mizban Khidr.[74]

Woods: Can you tell me something about the Mujahideen-e-Khalq operations, and their efforts around Baital and the battle of Qurnan? It sounds like this was a pretty large fight—22 Mujahideen-e-Khalq combat groups engaged inside Iran with some 15 Iranian brigades, that's a really large force. Would you tell us more about this?

Hamdani: There was definitely an opportunity that Saddam tried to seize for Mujahideen-e-Khalq because they just wanted to liberate Iran, while at the same time letting Iraq liberate its own territory. It is the same method used as with the Kurds. Saddam simply used them. Mujahideen-e-Khalq operations also served to get back at the Iranians for the way they used the Kurds up north against Iraq. The Mujahideen-e-Khalq was a good and well-trained organization. I have seen them more than once, in more than one mission. They have extraordinary training and are prepared as a standard army. They have experts with whom they train abroad and then return. They also have 20 percent females. You almost think it is a part of a European army, as far as the educational levels. They have excellent, educated members, the female part is prominent, and they are distinguished by being organized and courageous at the same time. The problem [in 1988] was that they went a little bit too far from their objective, all the way to Kermanshah. At this point, the Iranians could amass 15 Pasdaran brigades for defense and strike back against them. Here they were isolated [from Iraqi support] and were treated as traitors.

Discussion Ten

Foundations of the Iraqi Military and Saddam's Detrimental Influence—Hamdani's Effort to Improve Iraqi Military Culture—Questioning Military Orders and Planning—Lessons Learned from the Iran-Iraq War—The Fight to Follow the War and Saddam's Perception of Victory and Warfare

Hamdani: The army adopted the British style. They laid the foundation for us at the state level. I mean for us the British laid the foundation of a new state like Iraq. However, the presence of a [personality] like Saddam did not allow strong personalities to emerge, which weakened the army at the strategic level. I mean we had capabilities, good officers, and professors to teach us, but the nature of Saddam's leadership would not allow strong personalities [at the highest levels, because they might have represented an alternative to his rule].

Saddam had a conspiratorial personality; he always conspired against the closest people to him because of his personal ambitions to dominate. Therefore, he believed that the army was a good power to conspire against. [Thus] he tried to undermine the army. One of my uncles, killed in an aircraft accident in 1971, told me then that Saddam had once commented to him, "The Iraqi army was the only force capable of conspiring against me. The only power we fear is this army will take over the party's leadership. The army is like a pet tiger." Therefore, he [Saddam] pulled out its eyes, teeth, and claws.

Murray: It seems instead of the teeth and the claws, he removed the Iraqi army's brain to the extent that he could.

Hamdani: That is right, and this brain is an expression . . . I mean the brain because he had this conspiratorial mind and the way he pulled out its teeth and claws was by not allowing it any strong personality with the sense of adventure that soldiers love. He feared such personalities.

Right before the last war [Operation *Iraq Freedom*, March 2003], Saddam refused to devolve any kind of authority to division or corps commanders in the command ranks of the Iraqi army. I had to try to convince Qusay that this was wrong and it was going to work against him. Saddam, I argued, should treat the commanders according to their ranks and personalities; he should give them authority and allow them to have a personality and that he should not terrify them, so that they could assume [their] responsibility. So what I used to do is write orders to my subordinates and tell them, "Act as you see fit and if you make a mistake, I will be responsible for your mistakes."

Murray: It strikes me that unlike too many Iraqi officers you built up a relationship with your junior officers of trust because you took care of them just to the greatest extent possible. This created the situation in the last days of the 2003 war where you ordered . . . the bridges to be blown and your subordinates refused because they felt that if they blew the bridges, Saddam would execute you.[75] The chief of staff saved your life.

Hamdani: I mean we had many mistakes because the security situation reached an unbelievable level. So I intentionally promoted a slogan and had every unit of the army write it on the wall, since I wanted others to understand it, directly or indirectly: "Security is for us and not against us." I wanted security to be on my side and not against me. Honestly, wherever I went I used to leave this slogan, support it, and give lectures. I even told President Saddam Hussein directly that we should promote the expression, "Security is for us and not against us." It got to the point that one of my colonels (a security officer) became known as "the shadow." I mean anywhere I went, he was right next to me. My idea was that if it exceeds the limits it will not turn against us; I mean it should be in my favor.

In the last few years when security became extremely tight, the security services would take even my personal car . . . my family car, on the pretext of inspecting it to make sure someone did not plant an explosive device, but they actually did this to plant listening devices.

Murray: Do you think one of the reasons why Saddam became suspicious of you in the mid-1990s was not just simply because you spoke your mind, but also because, from Saddam's point of view, you were "currying favor" with your own men or maybe even plotting against him, when in fact, from your point of view, you were only doing what a good leader does, which was to encourage two-way loyalty?

Hamdani: I feel that Saddam Hussein did not even trust his sons; he got to that point. Saddam knew me since I had spent 21 years with the Republican Guard, and you get to know someone after 21 years. I truly did not have bad intentions against Saddam. He knew how I felt and knew that I would never cause harm or plan a coup or be a member of any coup or anything like that. He knew I would never conspire against him, but I prayed to God for Saddam to die no matter how, naturally I mean. I had no intention to accomplish such an act, but I wished that God would put an end to his life in a simple way, where Saddam would not lead us to this disaster where we are at present.

Saddam gave me the chance to stay [with the Republican Guard] longer, and I think this was for a reason; he needed a capable individual at the highest level. At the same time, he used to consider me like a school, in which he could train his relatives to be better officers. One day Saddam asked me, "I have two division commanders"—they were from his family—"here in the corps. I made them join the staff academy and one of them even joined the military academy. Why didn't they turn out to be good officers like you?" My answer was, "Neither the staff academy nor the military academy makes the officer a good commander. A good commander is the one who invests his time in studying at the staff academy and the military academy at the high level so that he will be good. He uses the knowledge he acquires and adds it to his experience, his military experience. It is not the academy that makes him." Besides, if someone, like a soldier, is motivated to be a soldier and live like a soldier . . . professional and dedicated, this is the critical ingredient; it is not something that can be taught. Saddam could not understand this concept.

Murray: You said earlier that a professional military discussion was difficult and was often seen as an abuse of military regulations, because your military tradition does not differentiate between debating and disobeying in the development process for orders. It strikes me that in any effective military organizations, discourse and discussion and debate are essential in the planning and preparation of military operations. Will you explain what pushed you to be willing to debate with your seniors, and how you encouraged your juniors to debate with you in terms of developing military plans?

Hamdani: It is true that we grew up in a military school that understood that you had to shape the plan with your leaders. We understood that you needed commanders who could talk freely. But following the war with Iran, the political approach was introduced. The [political approach] deprived this generation from learning the right method and approach.

Officers learned not to talk to anyone since, as I earlier mentioned, the security [restrictions] went beyond all limits. But as for my responsibility toward my officers, I tried to stay faithful to what I was taught in school. I grew up knowing that one cannot achieve success unless one reaches [a professional level]. I was trying to replace fear with certainty; all that I worried about within my command was not to have my subordinates fear me, but to become convinced of the idea. This was the command atmosphere where I worked and where I was a follower of your Western school. Command must be achieved by convincing and not by forcing.

That is why I used to encourage my officers to reach this level, even though I was not always allowed to talk this way. I also wanted to compensate for the losses we were about to face [in 2003] because, if a soldier has no self-respect, he is lost. That is why I said that the American soldier is organized and respected. He gives you the impression that he respects himself as a human being with rights, while even my division commanders had no rights.

The corps commander before me used to refer, on average, 300 cases every month to the military court. That average dropped down to just three a month while I was in command, except for cases related to the [misuse of] government funds and so forth. The [military] prisons in [my] divisions and corps had no prisoners. I used to do routine visits to the headquarters of the divisions, brigades, and battalions. Most of the time, I focused on leadership at brigade and battalion levels, because it is the responsibility of the commanders to understand their troops and their staffs.

The way I looked at it, [the high number of court cases] indicated a weak leadership because they did not understand why certain soldiers behaved in the way they did. [Early in my command] I used to spend long hours inside unit prisons, because I wanted to know why this person was in prison; I mean the numbers [of prisoners] were unrealistic. When I went to a corps or division unit and found prisoners, I would turn to the commander and say, "It is your mistake, and he is not an animal." I would make them understand that they did not need this many [soldiers] in prison.

Murray: General, you make an interesting comment in your memoirs about the Republican Guard in the immediate post–Iran-Iraq War period. You were a member of what you called the "Republican Guard battle analyzing team." In discussing attempts to learn lessons from the war, you wrote, "Our weakest point was the issue of benefiting from expertise, which was not appropriate to the extent and depth of the Iraqi military experience." Are you referring to the politicized nature of the process where there was little interest in drawing insights from the long-term or the short-term combat expertise of the army?

Hamdani: As a matter of fact, there were many lessons that we learned. But what really surprised me was to see so many people bluffing. I mean everyone tried to present himself as if he were the best in this field or that one should credit him for a particular event. Lessons were concluded and confirmed, but not at the right level or required depth.

In the final battles of 1988, the Iraqi army truly reached a high level [of performance], but at a very high cost . . . major losses. The biggest lessons we were supposed to learn were that future wars should not have as many sacrifices as this one. I made a point then by stating that we would need more heroes than martyrs in future wars.

[After the Iran-Iraq War] there was not enough time to reorganize the Iraqi army [to incorporate the lessons learned]. We started to reduce the troops of the Republican Guard and the army. But once again, Saddam's ambitions were too great. He did not provide us with the chance to absorb those lessons or reconsider [our] combat ideology (or doctrine), or to develop it and so forth. Saddam behaved as if his life as a human being would not last long enough to [wait for the] reorganization of his army; he was looking for another target so that he could reach a higher level by attacking Kuwait.

By the end of 1988 and beginning of 1989, he even thought of moving the Republican Guard to Jordan or Syria to [prepare to] fight Israel.

Woods: Was he so confident after 8 years of war that he wanted to take on the Israelis before his forces could recover?

Hamdani: Yes. After [the Iran-Iraq War] Saddam started to feel that he was the national leader for all the Arabs. Many started to think of Saddam as the one who had won the war. He had an unreal ambition. He started to think of himself as one of those leaders in Arab history with imaginary dreams and objectives.

Think about it: the [Iraqi] army had fought for 8 years and Iraq was economically drained. Wouldn't you give it some time, 5 or 6 years, to revive? But 5 months is a different story. This goes to underline the extent of ambition and what [a country with] ambitious leadership can do. Saddam saw this great victory as something he alone had achieved, and all the great losses only proved this fact.

Woods: How much of Saddam's rhetoric about war toward Israel or the liberation of Jerusalem was real? You just implied it was real, but how much was it just talk used to rally non-Iraqi Arabs to his banner?

Hamdani: In addition to the fact that he wanted to become that leader, he also had the confidence that he could accomplish this mission and eliminate Israel. I mean he believed his own stories since he used to conceal the many negative details and bring out only the positive ones. He expressed this confidence that he could accomplish this goal [of destroying Israel] in many meetings I had with him. He accused the Arab states of being weak and cowards for not joining him in making this decision.

Murray: It strikes me that Saddam's definition of war embodied a romantic picture of the warrior as the individual, and everything we know about modern war, as opposed to medieval war, was missing. It appears that to Saddam, he was simply a warrior from Tikrit fighting against the world. He seems to have completely missed the fact that modern military effectiveness, even for the Iraqi armed forces, depended not on individuals, but on teams.

Hamdani: That's right. I can add to this point and say that for his whole life, Saddam could only imagine war as a tribal conflict or like the conflict between Alexander the Macedonian and the Persian King Darius, or the conflict between Salah Ad-din and the Crusaders. I mean this was his concept of war, which did not adapt to modern times. He was always thinking of himself as a kind of Genghis Khan, Hannibal, or Alexander. He had a picture of these tribes or armies fighting with the sword. Saddam never actually realized that there was a huge difference between modern war and ancient war. [In modern war], there are other implications, political implications, international lines that you just cannot cross. Since I could not confront him too directly, I once told Saddam, "Most of our commanders looked at the war from the tribal perspective, more one-on-one warfare and not the bigger picture of modern war or today's war." He refused to listen.

Discussion Eleven

Stories of War Heroes, 1973 to Operation *Iraqi Freedom*— Saddam's Misunderstanding of Warfare—Hamdani's Recognition of U.S. Strategy in 2003—Understanding One's Enemy

Woods: Tell us some stories about the great soldiers who worked for you, some of the things that happened to them during the 8 years of war with Iran. I would like to hear about some of the men you considered heroes.

Hamdani: The war definitely killed many heroes. The Iraqi army had many true heroes at the level of the soldier, the noncommissioned officer, and other ranks. The majority of heroes, who used to take the blame for bad situations, were killed with a high percentage of heroes. . . . Here are some stories.

In the October 1973 Arab-Israeli War, there was a battalion commander named Major Abd-al-Hadi Ahmed Al-Rawi. He was a tank battalion commander, a battalion under the Iraqi 12th Armored Brigade. He realized at a certain point that his battalion had suffered so many losses from the Israelis that his troops had stopped their advance. In order to motivate his men and prove his fearlessness toward the enemy, he advanced with his tank as far as he could, until he entered the Israeli positions . . . with the Israeli tanks. He continued firing until his tank was destroyed by Israeli fire to provide an example to others that they must advance with courage.

Another story from the 1973 war concerns a first lieutenant named Taha from the commandos [Al-Maghawir]. He led a commando company and fought the Israeli tanks with all the weapons he had. He realized that our tanks were suffering major losses because of Israeli aircraft and the new American missiles [either Maverick or tube-launched, optically tracked, wire-guided missiles], which Israel used for the first time.[76] These missiles destroyed a considerable number of our tanks. I mean the situation was not in our favor. Taha advanced along with a small group toward one of the Israeli tank battalions at night. He surprised them and was able to destroy more than one tank. The Israelis were defeated in this particular tank operation.

I recall a sergeant, one of my tank commanders during the 1973 October war, who was very brave.[77] While we were still advancing, a formation of the Israeli Super Mystère aircraft [Dassault Super Mystère B.2] attacked us. These French-made aircraft fly at a low altitude. The Israeli pilots were very courageous and flying low enough that I was able to see the pilot's helmet from my tank. I saw the pilot because he was at the level of my tank's machinegun. That is how low he was flying. So this Israeli jet hits one of my tanks with its weapons. I noticed that the whole tank was on fire. I saw this sergeant, whose name was Hamid Shahin, get out of his burning tank. His right hand was destroyed. He was wearing a long-sleeve shirt so he wrapped his arm inside his shirt. I mean his hand just got cut off, and yet he still got something with his good hand to try and put the fire out.

In that war, I witnessed many heroic scenes of Syrians and Israelis. Truly many members of the Syrian and the Israeli armies were courageous. We should always admit the courage of our enemy.

During the war against the Kurdish insurgencies in 1974–1975, there were many acts of heroism, to the point where it is impossible to mention all of them; I mean scenes from all the parties, the Iraqi army, and the insurgents. One time, a group of Kurds crossed in front of my tanks and, not thinking, stopped to face my tanks with only their rifles. One of my tanks was moving forward and a Kurd shot the driver in the head with one shot. The tank kept moving, although the driver had been killed. The Kurds were still there and I had no other choice but to kill them, but at the same time, I respected them for their courage. To stand up against a tank with just a Kalashnikov, or a simple weapon, this takes great courage and dedication.

Murray: It strikes me again . . . that Saddam never understood that his enemies were men just like Iraqis. To Saddam they were always dehumanized as the Persian monsters or Israeli cowardly monsters, et cetera. He was always underestimating the nature of his American opponent or, as Saddam once described them, "the cowardly Americans who couldn't take 50,000 dead in Vietnam."

Hamdani: He was not a military man, otherwise if he were . . . If he had been a military officer, I mean, he would always have appreciated and respected that different perspective of his enemy.

Another heroic scene from the 1974–1975 Kurdish insurgencies was when a military engineer platoon commander moved in the lead of my tank company. The idea was for them to detect the mines, so that we could keep moving. The majority of this platoon was either killed or wounded by mines and sniper fire. The [engineer] commander was wounded from a gunshot in his neck. So he bandaged his neck and continued clearing the mines in front of my tanks until he reached the point where after much heavy bleeding he died. He got my tanks across that minefield and fulfilled his duty to me.

Yet another heroic story, also from the Kurdish insurgencies, concerns a platoon defending in a rocky area. They had a 360-degree perimeter in a mountain area to cover. At one point, a Kurdish force attacked this location with Iranian artillery support. This platoon continued to resist to the point where, although they were all wounded, they kept fighting. It took a while for their backup support to arrive. By the time we arrived, we could see the large number of Peshmerga casualties. When we finally made it up to their mountaintop position, the only ammunition this entire platoon had was one or two grenades. However, they never thought of surrender or anything like that. They resisted to the end.

During the war with Iran, we had thousands and thousands of heroes. It is truly hard to count. So many fought and most died during the war; they fought—starting at the level of the individual soldier to the high-ranking commanders level—fought under great political pressure and physical circumstances. They fought as if their action could lose the war and still they fought beyond heroism. Most of them were killed in this war.

I cannot mention everything, but there are literally thousands of stories about these people. At the same time, the Iranians displayed incredible acts of heroism, especially at the beginning of the conflict. The Iranians were courageous and determined to advance inside our lines, despite our superiority in tanks and artillery. I mean we were fighting up close and saw many Iranians fight without fear of anything. It was almost a funny story, you know, because in tank battles sometimes you had the Iranian infiltration, or you had the human wave attacks. Literally sometimes, you could see the Iranian infantry mixing with the Iraqi tanks, literally walking between our tanks. They showed tremendous will and dedication for sacrifice and courage to execute these kinds of attacks. Moreover, they were also tolerant of pain. I used to see their wounded being incredibly tolerant to pain.

What is sad is that we had heroes who survived the war, but they were dismissed by Saddam because he accused them of something or another.

Woods: Because they had become popular or perhaps become a political competitor to Saddam?

Hamdani: Well, I really don't know why exactly. Ali Hassan Al-Majid was behind relaying this message, which resulted in the issuance of the execution orders. But it was Saddam who approved them. General Bareq and General Aslaj . . . General Juwad As'ad . . . all these generals were accused of not fulfilling their duty in combat. General Juwad As'ad . . . I have never seen anyone as courageous or heroic as this one.

We had other excellent commanders in this war: General Salah Abboud and General Ayad Khalil. . . . We had many good and excellent division commanders, men such as General Riyadh Taha, the 12th Division commander. But they did not get their chance for an honest evaluation.

During the 1991 war, we also had many heroes, who are hard to list; I listed them in my book. In the 2003 war, the last war, I had a tank battalion commander; his name was Lieutenant Colonel Qais. He fought to the last moment, when the American forces started to cross from Al-Yousfiyah Bridge near Karbala. I knew we were not going to be able to succeed, but I realized we had to make one last try. The mission went to the 10th Armored Brigade; it was to counterattack the American forces.

The American units headed toward us one after the other. At around 2:30 in the morning I located the battalion commander in his tank, Lieutenant Colonel Qais. I briefed him by flashlight and explained his mission to him. I said, "Qais, the enemy has crossed the Euphrates River and I know it is a tough mission, but once daylight comes, the helicopters will attack us. If we can push them back across the bridge then maybe we can even demolish the bridge.[78] Do you understand the mission?" He replied, "Yes, sir." And when exchanging salutes he said, "The Staff Lieutenant Colonel . . . Martyr Qais," and he was killed like a martyr not even an hour later. I wanted to get his body back along with seven other injured but could not. Finally, they brought me his rank, which I kissed and kept.

I also had a captain who was the reconnaissance company commander. He made sure I had accurate information. He would dress up like a civilian and track the movement of the 3ᵈ Infantry Division. He would advance along with it and send me information about the progress of the V Corps and the 3ᵈ Infantry Division, whether they advanced or not. He used to get close to them. Even when he moved, I could communicate with him. He had a GPS [global positioning system] on his motorcycle, and he would transmit the location and the movement of this force to me at all times. He was killed after the war.

Murray: This story raises a question in my mind. Clearly, General Hamdani, you understood that U.S. forces were going to come through the Karbala Gap. In earlier discussions with Kevin Woods, you said this was because you had picked up on the establishment of an American logistic center outside Najaf around 21 March 2003. Was this activity picked up by Iraqi special forces or the reconnaissance officer you just described? This seemed to be the key factor in your understanding that the Americans were coming from the south and not the west.

Hamdani: Well, I understood the American attack plan for many reasons. First of all, I understood the American military tactical mind, since they always adopted maneuver. So first of all, I understood the American military mind.

Then, according to the reconnaissance patrol of my captain, we knew the Americans had stopped there at Najaf. So they told me that they stopped at An-Najaf to establish supply depots. After some analysis, I knew they were going to need time for reorganizing and that this stop was necessary. I wanted to track the movement of the American 4ᵗʰ Division in the sea on its way to Kuwait, since Turkey did not give it permission to enter. We thought the III and V Corps could not go any further toward Baghdad, until they got backup forces from the 4ᵗʰ Division. I mean it was only a matter of making the connection. If I were in General Wallace's place, I would not have been able to advance for more than 3 or 4 nights, unless I reorganized as far as the fuel, ammunition, and reinforcements with the arrival of the 4ᵗʰ Division. I mean I could not head to Baghdad, if I could not keep up the momentum of the attack. Therefore, I would have waited for the 4ᵗʰ Division to get closer to me. This was within the operation's logic.

AN IRAQI MILITARY PERSPECTIVE   **99**

Besides, the operational logic suggests there was one main mobilization area and that was Kuwait. The political situation in Jordan was not favorable; Jordanians would only allow one force to hide in Jordan that definitely did not exceed the size of a brigade. But a main effort composed of armor; it could not be in Jordan, since the political situation in Jordan is not strong enough for this, while Kuwait gave the opportunity, especially given their bitterness at Saddam's invasion.

So there were many indications that the main effort was going to come from the south. I was following the situation on the map and analyzing every move. If I were in the place of General Wallace, where would I go? What kind of attack plan would I have? The tanks always operate outside the urban area. I mean the desert area is better for tanks and we did not have a defense along the Euphrates axis. Therefore, this was better for V Corps' movement. So it is just the application of operational logic based on previous experience to think through what I would have done if I were in his place!

Woods: I told General Wallace, the former V Corps Commander, of your story and he said, in a very joking manner, that he was almost disappointed because it makes him seem less "brilliant" than people think, because you so adeptly figured out his plan.

Hamdani: In 1991, I expected the XVIII Airborne Corps to move towards Hafr-al-Baten according to a maneuver plan. That was the prediction I actually presented to Saddam, but everybody thought this was just science fiction. I was studying my enemy, reading his doctrine, and asking myself how they might do daily operations. Knowing the doctrine of your enemy gives you a better analysis of things. I came to these conclusions from my study of the American military mind. So this issue does not require as much brilliance as followup and getting to know the mind of the enemy, how they think, how their military mind analyzes issues, and how they apply it. So when I announced that the Americans were going to come and attack An-Nasiriyah, Saddam and his circle started questioning this and would not believe me. Because 95 percent of what I told them happened, Saddam asked me how I knew [laughing].

My analysis of the situation had nothing to do with brilliance, but two things; first, you have to understand the mind of your enemy. You need to understand his mind and doctrine. His mentality, his values, and the way they fight and doctrine. The culture and education of its commanders, because the more educated they are, the deeper will be their maneuver.

Finally, if you have experience, you can apply it to the other side and reach some conclusions. But the problem is that if you do not, you will be surprised. The truth is that war requires some brilliance that does not have to be extraordinary. Once you face reality, you can come to "brilliant" conclusions.

Murray: It's also an issue that not only amateur field marshals like Saddam, but most military commanders think simply of the enemy as this gray force—an enemy who will do what you want it to in terms of your own plan of maneuver. A first-rate commander always understands that the opponent is a living, breathing opponent who, as we say, gets a vote. Your adversary can always do something entirely unexpected.

Woods: A friend of mine once told me that, in a variation of a Sun-Tzu quotation, "Before you can defeat your enemy, you have to respect your enemy, and that is respecting him as you respect yourself." Respect in this case is not a moral decision. It is just that you must respect your enemy, if you ever hope to defeat your enemy.

Hamdani: Very nice! "Respect your enemy before you respect yourself, if you hope to win." We Iraqis have to admit that the American army showed courage in the last approach operations. Honestly, the Americans fought with such courage, zeal, and discipline and carried out the plan . . . which was not easy, since they were always moving and many of their soldiers fought with courage.

The American Army is fighting using an unusual counterguerrilla war method for the last 4 years that would make any other army collapse. But the American army is still holding there, which underlies that this is a great army that has wonderful training and excellent officers. There is an exception for every rule, but in general, the American army has proved for the last 4 years that while the Soviet army would have collapsed and any other great European army would have collapsed, they have not. Four years of fighting and the American soldier is still disciplined and zealous, and bears his losses, and this is a unique characteristic of this army. And I say this not out of courtesy, but I would hate to see the Americans leaving this area defeated, because they do not deserve to be defeated, but politics will not be fair to the American army.

Discussion Twelve

1990s Military Planning against Iran — Historical Explanation of Iran-Iraq Conflict — Religious and Ethnic Elements — Economic and Regional Aspects (Persian Gulf) — Shatt al-Arab — Ideology, Ba'athism, and Khomeini — The Present Conflict and Iranian and al Qaeda Influence

Woods: General Hamdani, over the last couple of days we have been talking about the events in the 1980s, the Iran-Iraq War, its lessons, and your impressions of what happened. Today, I would like to roll that discussion forward and ask about what the Iraqi military learned and more specifically what, if anything, the Iraqi military tried to implement in the 1990s regarding the defense of Iraq against Iran, based on your wartime experiences.

Hamdani: At the beginning, obviously, there were plans we laid out after 1988–1990, before we engaged in a war against the United States. There was then a second phase after 1991 until 2003, when our capabilities weakened. But please allow me to explain what the nature of a war with Iran would have been like.

First of all, we need to examine the nature of the war we are interested in, the Iranians as a nation, Iran's leadership, and the force centers in Iran. The Iranian people consists of several old Asian nations. At the time it consisted of a mix of several Asian ethnicities and groups. The Persians form a majority of 54 percent. There are also old nationalities like the second largest population group, the Azeris. Then there are the Baluch, Kurd, and Arab populations. There are some other minor nationalities that live in Iran. Iran experienced economic expansion at certain times and attracted other populations. So the Iranian population consists of several nationalities similar to the Iraqi population, but it is more complex.

In general, the original religion in Iran was a pagan one, where people worshiped fire, before Islam, as well as the religions of Zoroastrianism and Manichaeism. These were the basic religions. There were also a small percentage of Jews and Christians. When Islam arrived more than 1,400 years ago and spread throughout Iran, it spread by force and not *dawa* [invitation], and that is how the Iranian nation became Muslim. Until the year 1600, the main sect was the Sunni. With the emergence of Ismai'il Al-Safawi, many Arabs adopted the Shi'ite doctrine like the Persians who followed them. That process was completed by 1750 when 70 percent of the Muslim population had become Shi'ite. After 1750, with the rise of Ismai'il Al-Safawi, and the creation of the belief of the 12 imams, that was a turning point of the Sunni population to the majority being Shi'ite. The biggest factor was the emergence of the Safavid dynasty during the Nadir Shah's era in 1734, when he invaded Iraq.[79]

At that time, there were two major invasions of Iraq; the first one in 1626 and then 1734 by Ismai'il Al-Safawi. Both invasions aimed at restoring the ambition of the old Sassanian population at the same level, but under new leaders.[80]

The next phase began with the conflict between the Persian and Ottoman empires. This happened under the cover of the conflict between the Ottoman empire, which occupied Iraq, and the Persian empire, represented by the Safavid dynasty. It started in 1538 when the Battle of Préveza [Northwestern Greece] took place.[81]

There were many sensitive considerations regarding the borders between Iraq and Iran that resulted from this 1538 Persian-Ottoman conflict and have continued until this day. Therefore, we always noticed that, whenever the Persians have moved over the past 2,500 years until now, they always move toward the west, toward Iraq.

So why would Iraq be the most attractive [area] for Iran? Most of central Iran is a desert. This great desert and the Zagros Mountains are not arable. So what is left is the flat and open land by the Tigris and the Euphrates rivers, which became the main food basket for Iran.

Although have I spoken at great length about this background, it is so we can understand the roots of the conflict between Iraq and Iran. Maybe I went a little bit too long, but I wanted to explain the starting point of the conflict between the two nations.

Woods: No, in fact, you hit on all the right things. I think we could describe that history as the foundations of Iran's strategic culture. It helps explain how they might view the problems of today. What influences, out of the history that you just surveyed, do you think are most important today?

Hamdani: That is correct. At the strategic level, religious conflict had considerable influence, including its religious impact. This religious conflict revolves around the fact that Iran established its Shi'ite doctrine and has attempted to spread it throughout the entire area, especially the Arab regions. Remember that their first saint is Imam 'Ali, whose tomb is here in Iraq. Therefore, they considered it the focus of their religious thinking, a religious center, so in the Iranian mind it should be the center of the Shi'ite doctrine.

Most of these Shi'ite saints and their children lived in Najaf, Karbala, Baghdad, and Samurra. The remainder of the tribes of the most important followers of Imam Ali are located in the surrounding areas, you know, Basra, Baghdad, Kadhimiyah, and Samarra—the golden shrine.

If we look back, we can see that Iran supported those people against the pan-Arabism represented in the Umayyad State.[82] Therefore, they believed the rulers of Shi'ism or the family of the Prophet should be located in Iraq. So this Sunni dominance is just a temporary phase for these supporters and therefore, this religion's radiance center should be in Iraq. Moreover, they believe this religion should be the pillar of Islam, and not just in Qom, but also in Najaf. This division is just a temporary phase and Iraq should be the center of Shi'ite doctrine.

These places, Najaf and Karbala, are considered the center of Shi'ite doctrine as well as other doctrines and therefore, the Iranians consider that the Sunnis have stolen these ancient areas. They believe that the Sunnis should be eliminated and that if the Sunni control a Shi'ite area, this could occur only by force or else the Sunnis should convert to the Shi'ite doctrine. Only 150 years ago, the percentage of Shi'ites did not exceed 10 percent in Iraq. Seventy-five years ago, their percentage increased to 40 percent. They were about 55–60 percent during the last war [2003].

The reason for this increase in the Shia numbers in Iraq is because the Ottoman state was Sunni, and it weakened. Therefore, the spread started through the religious institutions of Iran. Just for comparison, the Shi'ite institutions are similar to the Catholic Christian system, while the Muslim Sunnis are closer to Protestants.

In true Islam, there is no institution; the Sunnis have no religious institution that programs, plans, and directs them, while the Shi'ite system is an institutional one with a head, various divisions, and specific funds.

The origin of Shi'ite doctrine and the fashion in which they established their doctrine was through worship of the grandchildren of the Prophet Mohammed. Therefore, the Shia considered these grandchildren as more holy than the other prophets. In fact, they started considering these descendants more holy than the prophets. After that, and since it exists in Islam, they believed that the Messiah is one of God's miracles. He ascended to heaven and came back again. Therefore, they replaced the Messiah with the twelfth imam, whom they considered the Messiah or the Mahdi. This is their doctrine. They replaced Christ with the Mahdi, the twelfth imam who was between heaven and Earth according to God's instructions to the Mahdi, which is the Messiah. Their Messiah leads to their current imam: Khomeini or, now, Khamenei. Therefore, there is no debate, when it comes to anything holy.

For them, the Mahdi adopted the same story of the Messiah that we have in the origin of Islam. They replaced the Mahdi's issue as being the most important, and he is the one who will appear on the day of resurrection, not the Messiah.[83]

Murray: It seems to me what we have here is the borderland that goes back to Rome and Persia for 600 years; this is the borderland where armies fight back and forth. This contested region is followed then, of course, by the Persian and Turkish empires: what results from that is the split between the Shi'ites and the Sunni. Iraq is in the middle and of course it has always been a center of civilization. But perhaps a better description is that it is a place where civilizations transfer ideas back and forth and contest with each other.

Hamdani: That is why the Sassanids originally entered Iraq. They conquered Iraq easily. After the invasion of Islam, it turned these secular interests into religious ones, but the reality is that they remained the same reasons as before.

Woods: So to what extent is the modern state of Iran driven by these historic forces or the religious motif?

Hamdani: The main motif is religious. The second motif is economic. The strategic culture issue you mentioned, since culture represents the nation, the Iranian nation expresses its strategic culture through its Shi'ite doctrine.

As far as the strategic issue, Iraq has been a competitor throughout history regarding the Gulf. Therefore, the entire Gulf area would be in the hands of Iran, should the Iranians control Iraq. The old history of Iraq indicates that this area was a theater for conflict because the Persians and ancient Iraqis were fighting at the time when Bahrain and Qatar used to be outposts for the ancient Iraqis. They have Iraqi roots. If we look at the royal Bahraini and Qatari family, we realize they belong to the same tribes in Iraq.

This area is an elevated dirt area and the deep water is close to the east coast of Iran. Therefore, the navigation lines for the old ships passed by the west coast, which gives better opportunities for fishing and pearl hunting. All of this happens along the west coast. As for the east coast, first, it is high, while the water is deep here; the deepest it can be close to the coast, while it is less deep along the west coast where it is shallow.

Historically, the Strait of Hormuz was under Persian control; the Iranians benefited from this only later on, but [historically] it remained under Iranian control. Iran had no interests beyond the entrance to the Gulf area at the time and therefore, there were no problems. Beginning around 1600, the silk trade was critical to the area. The silk trade starts at Afghanistan to the north of Iran and goes all the way to Europe

The second issue that affected the conflict with Iraq was that the silk trade line had the Tatars between Europe and us and the Turks. At the same time, British seapower started to emerge, and the British tried to reach an agreement with the Persians. They were worried that the silk trade might slip from being under the British control, not to mention their desire to protect their occupation in India. Therefore, in the 17th century, there was an agreement between the Iranian Persian governor and the British within the larger international competition in the region. At this time the international conflict shifted to the Gulf region and involved the French, Portuguese, Dutch, and British.

This issue recurred on a large scale following the oil discovery after World War I. The first area where oil was discovered was in southern Iraq, in Abadan, which was originally Iraqi territory, as well as Al-Muhammarah. This area is Ahwaz, which is ancient Iraqi land with an Arab population.

So the international interests divided the land. The British focused on Al-Muhammarah, while Iran took over Abadan in anticipation of future considerations. In the midst of all this, the Shatt-al-Arab issue emerged. This is the water channel that leads to Abadan. The British oil trade was tied to it.

Among the treaties to settle the border issues between Iraq and Iran was the Ard Roum Treaty in 1913.[84] It specified that Iraq should receive the Shatt-al-Arab in full, except for the east bank that should be given to Iran. The Ard Roum treaty occurred 5 years prior to the collapse of the Ottoman empire in 1918.

Murray: It strikes me that in terms of the 1980–1988 war, one has a change of focus from the traditional competition over Iraq proper. The real issue was the Iranian desire to control the Shatt al-Arab and Iraq's ability to export oil.

Hamdani: In general, the same history and tendencies, where the Persian empire was mostly interested in the north of Iraq, from 1980–1988 occurred. Nevertheless, their interest shifted toward the sensitive southern region, maybe because of the discovery of oil.

In 1937, a treaty was concluded between the Iraqi and Iranian governments to divide the borders, including Shatt al-Arab.[85] Shatt al-Arab was divided in half where the deep line is called the Thalweg line that delineates the line between

Iraq and Iran. The geographical problem of this issue is that Shatt al-Arab, and due to the Thalweg line and the river, would take land from the Iraqi coast and add it to the Iranian coast. I mean that Iraq started to lose territory as time went by. The normal course of the river changes when water spins during flood season. It takes from the Iraqi lands and adds to the Iranian side.

Another problem occurred when the British gave Bubiyan Island to Kuwait, which almost blocked Iraq from the sea. The ancient conflict started all over again about Iraq's sea passage through the Gulf. This is one of the other strategic factors among the religious, economic, and strategic ones.

The other problem was demography, the population issue. During invasions or during visits to the region, Persians started to settle in the center of Iraq. There developed a mixture of populations, where the Arabs live in the south of Iran in Arabistan [the Khuzestan area of Iran]. There are also the Arabs who settled in Baluchistan [southeastern Iran]. The Persians also entered from As-Sulaymaniyah area [Kurdish area of northern Iraq]; thus, the population in Al-Sulaymaniyah area became Shi'ite. What Dr. Murray talked about happened as far as the mixture of cultures and religions, as well as the strategic, economic, cultural, and demographic interests. The demographic interests are related to the cultural aspects of the competition.

The conflict continued during the great Shah era, which includes the young Shah.[86] It was about more than just the religious characteristics. Although the Shah did not support the Shia scholars in Iran, he supported the Shi'ite scholars in An-Najaf and Karbala. He hoped to destabilize the Iraqi government with the scholars, although he was against the scholars in Iran.

For example, the Shah supported Abd-al-Aziz al-Hakim and Ayatollah Mohsen Al-Hakim in Najaf.[87] They were great sources of trouble for the Iraqi governments in the 1950s and 1960s. They are originally Persian from the Tabtaba'i family from the Tabtab'ina region in the northern area of Iran.[88]

Murray: It strikes me that, mixed in with the historical background is the fact that on one side Khomeini had a particular megalomaniacal view of the 1980–1988 war, just as Saddam held a similar view of this war. A Sunni-Shia–run competition over a different version of a future caliphate?

Hamdani: No, let us talk about the Saddam era. If we look back at the period prior to Khomeini's arrival, the tension was originally pure Iranian nationalism. This was until Khomeini emerged. Then they used the pretext of religion to cover their strategic and economic objectives in the region.

When the Ba'ath came to power in 1968, the ideology was essentially Marxist. It had a realistic perspective on religion. The difference between the Marxist and Ba'ath ideology is that Marxism is international, while the Ba'ath is pan-Arab. Marx and Lenin (communists) spread their influence through all nations. The Ba'ath party is not international, but nationalist, at the level of Arab ethnicity, only. I just wanted to explain the difference between the Marxist and Ba'ath ideology.

The answer to what Dr. Murray raised: it was not a matter of Sunni or Shia. When Khomeini came in power, the state became an Islamic clerocracy; I mean Khomeini went back to Islam and its basis from a Shi'ite perspective. Iraq is a secular pan-Arab state, meaning it differentiates between religion and nationalism, and the religious and nationalist system.

So the conflict that took place during Saddam Hussein's era was between Khomeini and Islam on one side, and Saddam Hussein and pan-Arabism on the other. Thus, from the Islamic system and the Islamic ideology's perspective, Khomeini wanted to expand as long as there was a continuation of the Islamic world; I mean it became more like the communist system.

From the Ba'athist ideology, the religion issue was just a cover for an Iranian national issue, since this is a Persian conflict against the Arabs. It was not about Shi'ism, but it used Shi'ism as a cover and went back to the old conflict, the Arab-Persian conflict.

The core of the conflict came when Iraq considered the fact that Iran was under a religious cover; this was a national, historical, and cultural conflict. The Iranians had gone back to the Persian culture and were teaching that Iran was going to reoccupy Iraq, Syria, the Gulf countries, and even Egypt. Khomeini was trying to recreate the Persian empire.

Now, with the collapse of Saddam Hussein's regime, as a result of the war led by the United States, Britain, and some allies, the Ba'ath national movement ended and the nationalist determination to stop the spread of Iran disappeared. When the Shia emerged strong in large areas of Iraq, they no longer talked about this conflict in terms of Iranian propaganda. There was no longer a nationalist conflict, but now it was seen as a religious conflict.

As these last 4 years have passed, Iraqis, including the educated Shi'ites, have realized that a radical culture change had occurred in favor of Iran and its old nationalist interests. Therefore, the sense was there, but Iran has established a force through its Shi'ite parties and its support of Kurds like Talabani and so forth.

In other words, Iran had its own interests and acted according to them under the pretext of being against the Americans. The Americans must be drained so that if they lose and are kicked out of Iraq as a result of this conflict, there will not be any other force that can resist Iran and its spread into Iraq, Syria, and the Gulf area. But today, Iran has become part of the Iraqi politics. The Iraqi security ministries like the Ministry of the Interior, Ministry of Defense, and Ministry of the Internal Security are controlled through a union of religious parties, which as long as they are religious are extensions of Iran. So the pan-Arab Iraqis at present, whether they are Sunni, Shia, or Kurds, realize the current issue is our identity.

Thus, Iran was able, through American power, to eliminate that barrier and start to change the Iraqi identity through a Shi'ite culture in favor of the Persian culture.

Woods: Are you saying that the Arab Shia in southern Iraq now realize the influence of Iran and the underlying Persian political desires and are seeking more connection to their Arab identity?

Hamdani: Yes. What helped in this regard was the emergence of the Islamic Sunni scholars such as the Wahhabis and al Qaeda. They are culturally backward. Iran started to support these groups because a common enemy for both sides was the Americans.

Woods: So in your opinion, Iran's strategic objectives allow them to use groups such as al Qaeda and the Wahhabis, even though their ideology is antithetical to Shi'ism, in order to kick coalition forces out of their countries. Is that correct?

Hamdani: Yes, in fact, I did a study and recently presented it to the chief of staff of the Jordanian army and to the King's advisor on tribal affairs. I argued, "The Americans are now the barrier. . . . Iraq was the barrier, but now the Americans are. So, if this barrier is removed, it will not take the Iranian tsunami more than 10 or 15 years to invade the area"—just like the tsunami disaster that hit the Indian Ocean region. For this reason, it is in the Iraqi national interest to support the American Army in Iraq instead of fighting against it. That is what I intend to work for. I have talked with the Jordanian, Lebanese, and some Syrian intellectuals, Yemenis, Emiratis, and Qataris as far as supporting the American strategy in Iraq.

This is the core of the strategy understood by both the Iraqi nationalists as well as all sensible Arabs: The situation has changed from the time when the Americans came in 2003. We and they had different friends and different enemies. This has changed today. Those who were friends turned into enemies due to Iranian strategy, and the enemies who used to be against America now are becoming their friends. This is the nature of things at the strategic level and in big politics.

Woods: Regarding the issue of Persian-driven Shia expansionism, what is the impact on the Arab and Iraqi Shias? What is the reaction in southern Iraq?

Hamdani: Iraqi Shias have had a positive reaction. Initially they started to open up and talk about how they were isolated under Saddam and did not have much contact with the religious institutions, but then the militia forces started to hit them. In fact, I personally met with more than six major tribal leaders who were crying and saying, "We were deceived, Iran tricked us and tricked America; we have to be Iraqi nationalists again where our interest comes before the Sunni and Shia issue because, if not, we are definitely going to lose Iraq." And it's not only them, but also some Kurds. More than one Kurdish tribe leader has said the same thing. But today these nationalists don't have the power because of the militia and religious parties. For instance, one of the tribal leaders in the south who was an old Iraqi general told me, "In early stages of the war you couldn't discuss these kinds of things; we would try to object but it was a religious issue, like a religious umbrella and everybody rallied under it. Now, I have armed people who come to me and say, 'We need to mobilize to actually fight Iran and stop this influence.'" Everyone is fighting the religious scholars since they have ruined our country.

Murray: It seems to me that from al Qaeda's perspective, their plan for the long run was to shake up the situation and create this problem of Sunni-Shi'ite antagonism.

Hamdani: But the truth is that currently, the religious institutions are going to weaken here just like they did in Europe following the Middle Ages. This is because the current religious institutions do not represent a religion, but instead political interests. Everyone complains because they do not want a Sunni religious institution or a Shi'ite religious institution. Following the dark ages, religion weakened and the people separated from the churches in Europe and focused more on education.

The most hated figures in Iraq are the ones educated in religious institutions, whether they are Sunni or Shi'ite. Even in Iran they are starting to hate the scholars and institutions.

This is related to our issue now with regard to how to face the Iranians' attacks and anticipate them, because the influence of scholars has weakened. This is very different from the way it was when we first started the 1980 war with Iran, where they were considered holy. Today, people openly complain about the religious institutions in Iran.

Discussion Thirteen

Planning for an Iranian Adversary—Iranian Structure—2003 and Iranian Strategy—Ayatollah as Executive—Iranian Military Development and Capabilities—Missiles—Iranian Threat to Iraq and Infiltration—Internal Agents—Iraqi Counterinfiltration—Iranian Militias—Iraqi Military Developments since 1991—Cooptation of Tribes

Woods: Can you describe the military considerations your experience dictates when contemplating Iran as an adversary?

Hamdani: I will start at the level of the general staff of the army first, the higher level and how we looked at the beginning at the nature of the battle or the war that might have taken place.

Let us ask ourselves: What is our analysis of the nature of the hostile command we confront in Iran? Ayatollah Ali Khamenei is the head of the Iranian command pyramid. He is the top of the pyramid of all religious, civilian, military, and economic institutions.

He is like the Pope during the Crusades. From the European side, Gregory VII gave orders at all levels. This figure connects all the way down to the individual level. These institutions connect together during various phases. The Ayatollah is considered the great dictator of all the institutions. But a dictator who takes them to heaven, unlike Saddam Hussein who takes his people to hell.

For example, there is a connection between the Iranian state and the institution of the Iranian army. Mahmoud Ahmadinejad presently heads state institutions. However, since the Iranian revolution, it lies within the same structure as the army. This also connects directly with the religious institutions. There are the other institutions that are related to the students and lower-level institutions.

There is a double connection between the army and the head of state and Iranian Revolutionary Guard. There is also the Basij, the third form of ground forces, which falls under the government but has direct connection to religious organizations.

This shows you the complexity of the Iranian structure. The military may fall under the control of the current government under Ahmadinejad, but it also receives orders from the higher ranking Khamenei. Then there are special offices, for instance, the office for Iraq, which also is directly connected to Khamenei. The Quds force is one example. All of them are connected. The office dealing with Lebanon also connects to Khamenei.

Therefore, we must focus on the way Khamenei thinks, since he is the most important leader, and he is the main policymaker. The other leaders are nothing but for show. In fact, he is the main source of guidance, and there are no orders from any of those other leaders that do not come from Khamenei.

In May 2003, one month following the collapse of Saddam's regime, Khamenei met, through the Iranian office for Iraq, a number of the tribal military delegations, including a military delegation. They were mostly Iraqi Sunni and Shi'ite officers. Khamenei focused on the Sunnis and provided them funds to form an armed resistance against the Americans.

As I said, in May 2003, Khamenei met with the Iraqi committee that consisted of Iraqi tribal leaders, scholars, and some of the Sunnis. They had old Sunni military members and Iraqi military members and he offered them large amounts of money to create an insurgency. I know two of the officers who met with Ali Khamenei regarding this matter, and they told me about this incident.

So the Iranians tried to send large amounts of money to other parties, especially the Sunnis in Al-Anbar region, as well as other regions. . . . They focused on preparing a major insurgency against the American presence in Iraq. They spent a week at the Pasdaran headquarters and another week at the operations center. Ali Abd-al-Aziz al-Hakim was in charge of these Iraqi delegations; he brought them to Iran and provided them with the documents necessary to transit between Iran and Iraq.

While at the Pasdaran headquarters, the Iraqis were asked to explain . . .
about the American ground forces, about the Marine forces, and about the air
force, as well as the overall American offensive against Iraq. Their true intention
was to kill people, especially the Americans in Iraq, eliminate them, and then defeat them in order to gain control of Iraq.

Woods: Were these former Iraqi officers credible? Were their military
opinions respectable? What kind of units did they command?

Hamdani: They were former staff officers at the Ministry of Defense. But
let us get back to our subject. Despite the continued control of the Iranian military
by a religious command, it became much harder to remain loyal than it was 20
years ago when Khomeini came into power.

Woods: You mean the influence of an individual imam to send an Iranian
volunteer unit to the front had disappeared by the 1990s? What does this tell you
about the effectiveness of Iranian C^2? Has it improved at the operational level?

Hamdani: First, any instructions or guidance will still take a certain time
to get to the troops, since an Islamic scholar will still issue it. Khamenei is the only
one who decides any issue. When Khamenei signs or approves it, this will be holy
writ to those who must comply. Disobeying would be equivalent to disobeying a religious instruction. Even during the Iran-Iraq War, all the resolutions issued had to
be approved by Ayatollah Khomeini and then Ayatollah Khamenei in order for the
order to acquire the required holiness. This gave orders a spiritual quality. People
would obey, because they accepted the holiness. But this holiness started to weaken
day after day. It is much weaker today than before. The charm and influence of religious institutions on this subject have weakened.

Let us turn to the Iranian army. The senior leaders in Iran benefited from
lessons learned during the 8 years of war with Iraq. They have significantly reorganized their forces. At the same time, they have focused on long-term developments
such as missile systems, naval forces, and long-range weapons. As for the air force,
theirs is considered mid-size, but well trained. They have also focused on airborne
forces, paratroopers.

For instance, they learned from the Iraqi experience that it is hard for
an air force to destroy the enemy's mobile missiles. Therefore, Iran has focused
on mobile missile bases. As for the fixed or main strategic targets, Iran relies
for their defense on new Russian surface-to-air advanced missile systems like
the S–300.

At the same time, the Iranian army has developed to a level similar to that
of the level of the Iraqi army in 1990. The Pasdaran has become the regular army
and is now more committed and reliable. There is also the Quds force, the main responsibility of which is to interfere inside Iraq. The new Iranian army is being built
on a large, military industrialized base. At the present, the Iranian army mainly

concerns itself with defending Iran in general and maintaining the benefits of the Iranian policies in Iraq.

As for the navy, it has acquired the Chinese Silkworm missiles with ranges from 75 to 200 kilometers. But as you know, their main defense line is the Strait of Hormuz for the navy and Bandar Khomeini and Abadan in the Arabian Gulf. At the same time, they consider their nuclear reactors as one of the strategic targets that the United States can hit, and therefore, they want to defend them. This is why Iran is developing a missile called the Phantom for use in the Gulf. It cannot be detected and would be used to attack American ships in that area. As I mentioned before, the deep water lies near the east coast of the Gulf and, therefore, the Iranians rely on the antiship weapons and coastal weapons based on the assumption that aircraft carriers or battleships will have to get close to the coast.

The Iranians will also rely on speedboats with suicide bombers from the Revolutionary Guard, who are willing to carry out that duty. At the same time, the average width of the Arabian Gulf is only 270 kilometers. Therefore, if these small boats can reach 200 or 250 kilometers, they can strike from hidden areas and are suitable for defense against large warships.

Woods: What do you think the experience of the Iran-Iraq War taught Iran about surface-to-surface missiles? After watching Iraq's wars, many have argued that the Scud missile, for example, is a good psychological weapon, but not an effective one in military terms. Do you think the Iranians would agree with this "lesson"?

Hamdani: In fact, Iran is relying on missiles as a strategic weapon. It has adopted the same strategy as the Iraqi army in 1991. Iraq defied the Americans by striking Israel. Iran can defy the Americans by striking Saudi Arabia and the Emirates. They have a variant of the same type of missiles in the Shahab–1, Shahab–2, and Shahab–3. The Shahab–3 is one of the most dangerous missiles, since it can reach Israel. Israel will definitely have to rely on the same method it used against Iraq, where it depended on the Americans to strike the missile launch sites.

The Iranian military learned a lesson. During the 1990–1991 war, the U.S. force did not manage to destroy a single mobile Iraqi missile. Missiles such as the Al-Hussein struck Israel despite their short range. This was because it is hard to hit because it was mobile. There were more than 2,000 American air sorties against the Scud launchers and yet they did not manage to hit even one. Therefore, Iran has focused on the long-range mobile missile bases.

Regarding Iran's threat to Iraq, there is the Quds force that is currently spread across Iraq in different areas. Second, there are a large number of Iraqi militias related to the Quds force in this location [pointing to a map of southern Iraq as he speaks]. The Quds force has many communication points; Al-Basra, which is the Shalamjah area. If you look at this area between Majnoun and Shalamjah, we have Shalamjah and Ghzayyil area in this location and the infiltration points in Majnoun area, the areas starting from Jayzaboun toward Al-Amara and Al-Shihabi areas . . . and to Badra and Jaffan in these areas. Summar, here is Kut and here is Summar, these are the infiltration areas, and we also have the areas near to what they call Zain al-Qaws area near Khanaqeen; these are constant infiltration areas. Although these areas are currently protected by militias or even local forces, they get their salaries from the Quds force.

Woods: How did Iraq deal with such infiltration in the 1980s and 1990s?

Hamdani: We had counterinfiltration units. There were also troops along the border, but these infiltration points were difficult to control. We had a battalion of infantry for each major point. We used to leave a tank battalion deep in every location as a way to keep these areas secure.

All along Shatt-al-Arab, Iraqi naval infantry guarded the infiltration points such as Sida, Al-Fao, Salboukh Island, and an infiltration point here called Al-Kharroumiyah. There were approximately six main infiltration points the Iranians used constantly. That is why we had the naval infantry of approximately one division's size in charge of Shatt-al-Arab. These islands are muddy and full of orchards, so they are good for infiltration and crossing. The water area is also narrow, which makes it easier to cross and infiltrate. From the Iraqi side, there are branches of the main river that extend into Iraq. The largest one, for instance, we call Abu-Flous, is in Abu-al-Khasib area, where large Iranian boats used to cross and unload soldiers onto Iraq's territory.

We used to close the local canals in such a fashion that water can flow in, but through water barriers made of iron, boats could not cross, only the water, since this was necessary to irrigate the orchards. The irrigation happens with the ebb and flow of the tides; the flow reaches as high as 3 meters, while the water decreases to 0.5 meter with the ebb. So the Iranians used to infiltrate here, especially during the flow period. The flow period was the most critical period, and our troops were always on alert during this period.

This was in the Shatt-al-Arab area where the Tigris and Euphrates River meet. The area of Qitbah, for instance, was the crossing point for people from Al-Muhammarah [Khorramshahr] and Shalamjah, and therefore these areas needed to be strictly monitored. That is why we set up observation posts with radar to detect movement and signal that there are Iranian patrols in the area. Most of the infiltration came through this area. [See figure 4 in Discussion Four.]

Based on my expertise, we wanted to shut the seawater passages, not to mention using local militias to protect the vital areas and light and medium machineguns along the coast, so that we could tightly control any crossing site. This means there was an appropriate light and medium machinegun mobilization, and at the same time, we had mortars since the Iranians used to land boats or forces through Shatt-al-Arab.

These are some of the green areas including Al-Huwayzah; this one was the most dangerous one where they always succeeded in crossing the road between Basra and Amara. In the marshes area, and, although we used to place large numbers of troops here, the Iranians were still able to infiltrate.

But the Iranians could not infiltrate everywhere. There were established routes for water and ground movement. So we used to set up ambushes along these routes with floating bases, like floating bridges, and station an infantry squad on them with machineguns and RPG–7 launchers.

We also built observation posts as high as the highest level of plants so that we could monitor any movement by use of radar.

Woods: Can you describe the size of these infiltration routes? How many personnel or much military traffic could pass over them? A platoon? A company?

Hamdani: All sizes. In 1984, in this area, the Iranians were able to infiltrate two divisions. But after learning from our experiences and taking the measures I just described, the infiltration decreased significantly.

These areas have oil fields with many large dirt berms, roads, and intersections. They were protected directly by our troops. We set up an intense monitoring and protection system for them and, as a result, we stopped any major infiltration attack from using the oil fields, but we had to place a large number of troops there.

Murray: What were the most important infiltration routes in terms of threatening Baghdad?

Hamdani: The other infiltration point is Al-Teeb area in Bazergan and around the oil fields. These oil fields in Bazergan in this area . . . this area has a lot of swampy areas that facilitate the infiltration. These are also traditional criminal smuggling routes.

Murray: So the locals on both sides, they knew how and who got through these routes?

Hamdani: This is their lifestyle from then until now. It is the way they make a living. The other infiltration point they used is that these water channels are deep, of course, like Al-Jabbab River here.

Moreover, since the channels are deep, we used to guard the wings and use wire obstructions. For instance, when the water flows with speed, they will collapse, because the fast-moving water will push away the obstructions and the barbed wire. Therefore, we always had engagements because when the floodwater flows. . . . The problem we used to have in guarding the river routes (the Tigris River, especially in the Shaykh Saʿd area) was after a storm. Then, the current would become very strong. We protected the area by having forces on both sides of the river. They would string wire across the river. However, sometimes when it rains the current becomes so fast and so strong that it can destroy the wire obstacle. But when they were in place, they limited the infiltration by boat. So we worked hard to maintain the wire at all times.

The other critical area lies in the Badra and Jaffan area.[89] This is another valley that leads to the river down here, a valley where the water flows and an area with many shepherds and locals. As Dr. Murray suggested, smuggling was their job. We used to use troops and machineguns to block the valleys and when the water was shallow, we would plant antipersonnel mines.

This is a safe area because it is very rugged and hard to move in it, not to mention it is open, which makes it easy for the patrols to monitor it.

This area is called Kani Shaykh. They call it "death valley." These areas aided the infiltration of large numbers (up to regiment size) of enemy forces. It is an area of deep valleys that are hard to infiltrate at night.

Murray: Is there a connection between these routes and where you might attempt to make military advances with major units?

Hamdani: We have a saying for the infantry division: If a soldier infiltrates, so can a regiment.

Murray: I understand. However, are any of these infiltration routes also places where you could move armored or mechanized divisions in a more conventional way?

Hamdani: No, not really. As for the Iranians, they rely on the infantry to start everything. By that, I mean they have an infantry mentality. The Iranians are the most skilled in infiltration tactics. Ninety percent of the Iranian battles started as platoon infiltrations and grew to the battalion level.

Woods: Did you see any changes in the way the Iranians infiltrated in the 1980s from what you were seeing or expected in the 1990s? Do you think the Iranians learned the lesson that maybe relying only on infantry was not such a good idea? Did you have any indication that the Iranians were starting to mechanize these tactics and emphasize conventional forces like the Iraqi army?

Hamdani: You get to know their way of thinking after being engaged in a war for several years. I watched both sides and their maneuvers largely remained the same. The Iranians were at their worst when using armored forces in the classic maneuvering way. When I watched these recent Iranian maneuvers on TV, I could see that the tanks are always supporting the infantry and are not the main attack force.

Besides, they are currently focused on an airborne theory. They want to rely on using airborne units moved around by helicopters. However, you must have complete air superiority in order to adopt this method. Any movement of helicopters would be an easy target for the American enemy.

I am willing to sign a document stating that the Iranians are unable to use armored forces in the fashion that I understand they should be utilized. This is because of their mentality. I have always listened to their military dialogues. These latest examples of Iranian maneuvering exercises demonstrate that they still use armored forces in the old-fashioned way. By that I mean they focus on infiltration. They get their agents inside Iraq, establish communication between their forces and the ones on the inside, and then they start to expand in isolated locations. Soon they connect one location to another so that they can use them to build defensive barriers inside Iraq.

Pardon me, but let me give you another true story. One of our tank commanders once met with Saddam Hussein after a successful battle against the Iranians.

Now, this officer was not much of a professional, not well educated. Anyway, Saddam asked, "How were you able to achieve such a great victory and defeat the Iranians?" The commander replied, "Sir, it is because they are stupider than we are." This was an officer who was not afraid to say anything, but he was also known for not thinking before he spoke.

Murray: What did Saddam say?

Hamdani: He chided him and said, "How can you say that?" But nothing ever happened to him.

Back to the discussion of infiltration routes. The other infiltration point is in the direction of Shahda oil fields and Khamer and this leads to an area. There is a hill, very important.[90] The Iranians infiltrate from this area and move toward Khanaqeen, a high mountain area. The crevices help the infiltration in this area.

The other area, this is, of course, a main road that can carry large numbers of troops and from which we entered Iran; the main roads had armored troops. So we entered the areas we crossed, since we are armored troops; we crossed in this direction. These areas are good for the operation of armor. And regarding the Summar area, these are also conducive to the operation of armor. For the Iranians, they might have crossed their armor in phases that followed the initial battles, but in the early stages, they relied on infantry infiltration.

The other area that helps is the Dakh Mountains; they are critical areas for infiltration. The last area is Halabjah and Darbandikhan; the Iranians used these areas to infiltrate by us. The other areas are Penjwin[91] and Qal'ah Daizah. All mountains, these areas are just mountains. These areas are currently in the Kurdish area.

We talked about Haj Umran yesterday; Haj Umran was the main road. This road is critical since these are very rugged areas. Similarly, Saffin Mountain and Khosnaw area, and there is another road that leads to Taqtaq, crosses the Zab River, and goes toward Kirkuk.

Woods: Tell us about the counterinfiltration measures used along these rugged areas. What were your options?

Hamdani: From the beginning, we relied on two things: small light units, special forces and infantry, spread out along the border. Some of these far areas we only monitored because it was seldom continuous. This became a system, a full system. Just a small force would establish an overwatch point. Their focus was only on detection. However, behind them we had defensive posts and a defense line oriented along the parallel roads [see figure 10]. These were our secondary line of defense for infiltration.

Woods: Were these second line positions mobile or fixed? What kind of defensive line was this?

Hamdani: Both. There were fixed defense lines and there were patrols. These were defenses. This whole system consisted of defense areas. In this area, there were observation posts and defensive positions. These areas were under continuous observation. Some posts were actually artillery observation posts. Some areas were just focused on killing the infiltrators. Because of all the roads, it was not practical to establish a defense. It was a defense in depth.

Woods: Can you describe your understanding of Iran's military objectives, as it relates to the infiltration activity along Iraq's border?

Hamdani: First of all, the Iranians were never able to carry out deep penetrations, since they limited themselves to infantry infiltration. For example, it would take them 2 to 3 days to infiltrate before an attack would take place inside Iraq. By the fourth or fifth day, the infiltration would be joined by Iranian supporters inside Iraq. But they never succeeded in executing a deep infiltration, because they do not use large armored units. Their principle in using the armored unit is fixed to infantry support and not as a central force.

After 1992, Iraq started relying on our main forces to protect the cities from the Iranian infiltration and its supporters from the Badr Group and Peshmerga. So what happened is that we resorted to defending crossroads inside of Iraq and left the border areas because isolated confrontations were difficult.

What we did was to control the crossroads and, when an infiltration took place, the reserve force would follow the infiltrators and kill them. We did not defend the borders after 1992 strongly; we went back to monitoring the communication nets and the main cities, and we established a scientific system for monitoring, security, and intelligence along with local forces at the regiment or battalion level. Of course, the Iranian strategy changed after 1991. I mean the Iranian army was no longer coming into Iraq. The Iranians instead relied on infiltrators and trained militias affiliated with them.

What they did was they entered the cities to incite the people against Saddam's regime. This was the change in Iranian strategy; they wanted to instigate the cities against the Iraqi regime.

In response, we had to tighten our control over the cities. We focused on the security issues, intelligence and security. Occasionally we launched raids on the locations of the Iranian infiltrators, who wanted to cross into our land.

Woods: Do you believe this Iranian strategy continues today?

Hamdani: Regarding Iran's current strategy, I do not expect that there will be any direct Iranian intervention with armored forces or regular infantry forces. There is no need. The Iraqi Ministry of the Interior, the Ministry of National Security, the Ministry of Defense, and some of the current militias have this covered. So what they will do, in their current strategy, is supply these entities with the weapons, equipment, munitions, and machines, while at the same time appointing the commanders. At present, Iran has established the largest intelligence system operating inside Iraq.

Figure 10. **Map of the Kut-Sulaimaniyah border with General Hamdani's markings**

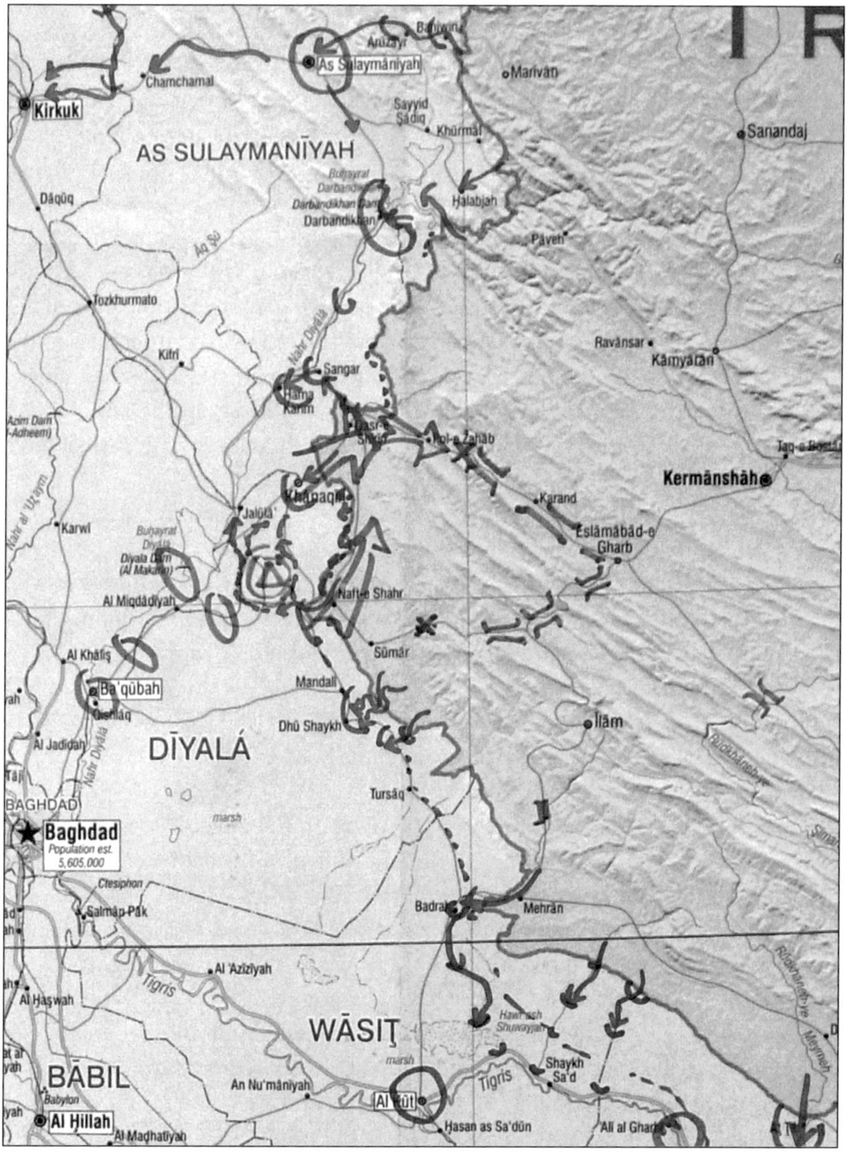

Source: U.S. Central Intelligence Agency, "Iraq," DI Cartography Center/MPG 802950A1 (C00519), 1-03. Red = Iranian infiltration movements. Blue = Iraqi defensive positions and movements. Green (in Iran) = theoretical Iraqi positions for potential mission and choke points.

For example, Adnan Palace is in the Green Zone. Yet there are five specialized and trained people working for Iran there. They meet Iraqi officials, they receive information, and send the main Iraqi Interior Ministry forces any place. These five members hold sensitive positions within the Iraqi government. They are like the top of the pyramid in Iraq. However, they direct the militias with the help of the Iranians, who have already infiltrated or Iraqis who were trained back in Iran.

Once the Shi'ite religious scholars control the entire system, they will be hard to stop. The religious scholars are spreading everywhere. You Americans even provide them with the support. However, these scholars are not well trained and what matters is identifying the key people. Once the key people are controlled, these people will become weak.

Woods: Returning to the period after the 1991 war, how did the Iraqi military change?

Hamdani: Our strategy relied on the following: first, expanding the intelligence system so that we would know every movement from the front lines to the headquarters. We set up ambushes based on this information. Groups of Iranians would come with weapons, give them to Iraqi sympathizers in the villages, and spend the night. The next morning we would set up an ambush with a small force and stop them.

The second phase was, if we could tap into their communications networks, we would discover when the Iranian agents would be arriving in the city or who they were going to meet with. So these disloyal Iraqi figures and leaders who were the cause of trouble would meet with the Iranians to plan followup meetings and launch a larger strike. Once they struck, the city would go back to normal.

We had a force that was always ready as a reserve force in every city.[92] If control were lost, the reserve force would block the city and then storm it. Pretty much all the major cities or the villages along the border had this system. It aimed at avoiding any kind of revolt within the cities.

Originally, you have to have a presence in the cities, a secure position inside the cities. Your success starts with your presence inside the city, and then you start to expand your security range in a way that you are aware of any issue in the city. You have a center that will stay strong due to the level of control and communications. So if the Iranians and their agents go in and start causing trouble or revolts against the regime, the center will remain strong.

This is the appropriate response because we did not expect Iranian regiments and brigades to arrive. We found infiltrators with weapons inside our cities, and they started causing trouble. So we decided that if we could hit the key communication points it would be good. Otherwise, these Iranian agents would get deep inside. That is why you Americans have to have a strong security center inside and forces able to block external forces at any time.

Murray: After the 1991 war, Saddam appears to have put far more reliance on the tribes for security. Were the tribes a critical component in terms of providing increased and more effective intelligence of what was going on?

Hamdani: In fact, he tightened the noncentral control of every one of the tribes, so that he could compensate for the lack of security forces after the Gulf War. The losses caused a kind of decentralization of parts of the intelligence system.

For instance, let us say you have tribe X. It becomes known to the regime that one of tribe X's clan members is secretly a rebel and works at one of the government centers. If this person gets arrested and admits he belongs to tribe X, the tribe's leader in this case will be punished. This is the first case. Now, the other case is if the tribe leader knows of this traitor in his clan and reports it to the government, the government will forgive him. It tells him, "It's up to you, you are the leader of this tribe and it is up to you to punish the rebels or not." This will prove the tribal leader's integrity. This method forced every tribe leader to tighten his control over his tribe. They were now acting out of fear and became most diligent.

Discussion Fourteen

Role of Religion in Iran-Iraq Conflict — Hypothetical Iraqi Offensive against Iran and Phases of Preparations — Iranian Influence in Iraq — Arabistan — Baluchs and Kurds — Air and Missile Strikes and Military-Industrial Complex — Younger Iranian Generation — Smart Weapons and Satellites — Terrain — Operational Objectives — Iranian Lessons Learned — Iranian Missile Deterrent

Woods: What role does religion play in the never-ending tension between Iraq and Iran?

Hamdani: The Iranians are all part of the bigger Islamic brotherhood community. Hizb Ad-Da'wa…Ad-Da'wa political party; this is kind of how one gets back to Iran. They have a system that is similar to an international force; it exists in all countries.

This clerical ideology, I mean it also includes the ideology of Sayyid Qutb, is destructive.[93] Like other ideologies, including communism, having everything controlled by a [clerical] scholar is destructive for civilization and progress. For example, Hamas was a creation of the Israelis.[94] The Israelis made Hamas, so that it could compete with Fatah [the Palestine Liberation Organization], but they lost control.

The United States provided much support, general support like logistic and financial, to the Shia to overthrow Saddam's regime. Unfortunately, the Shia never recognized or appreciated that support. They always maintained closer ties with Iran than with the United States, regardless of the kind of support provided to them by the West.

There cannot be an alliance between the future and the past. The ideologies of the religious parties always have a tendency to look toward the past. While the secular ideologies, like the United States, have a tendency toward the future. Therefore, they cannot possibly agree. Each is the opposite of the other. It is like they are back to back and going in completely different directions.

Woods: General, what I want to do this afternoon is to run a counterfactual war game. I would like you to describe for us what an Iraqi offensive against Iran would have looked like, if you had had benefit of the lessons of the past three wars and, needless to say, different leadership. What do you think the limits of military force in such a scenario might be?

Hamdani: This is a hard question. We are heading into the toughest part of our discussions over the past few days. It is a complex question and it involves many factors. In addition, Saddam Hussein only understood half the question in this issue—the use of force, but not its limitations.

So that we will not make the same mistake as Saddam Hussein, let me start with some wisdom from 2,500 years ago. Sun Tzu defined a long war as very difficult and commented that it would be a mistake to engage in such a conflict.

He wrote a work about the long war, a conflict between two countries. The first country is small, but has high technical ability and great power, yet a small population. The second country is weak, but it is big country with a large population. The long war happens when there is a conflict between these two kinds of countries.

The small country cannot afford to occupy the larger country and the larger country does not have the power to stop the small one.

Murray: It strikes me that the only way for Iraq to tackle Iran in any kind of military fashion was to first separate the religious regime from its people. A large component of any campaign would have to be psychological warfare and efforts to undermine the popularity of the regime. In fact, is this not what happened by 1988, where Khomeini was getting worried about his popularity and that is why he eventually stopped the war?

Hamdani: What Dr. Murray suggests is true. Any war aimed at Iran has to have preliminary phases.

As a preliminary step, we would have to get rid of the Iranian influence. We have to start any operation from a safe and strong base. A strong base we can rely on; it has to be strong and safe before we start, because you cannot start an offensive, if you have internal threats.

Of course, your troops have to be loyal to your cause, to your country; you cannot be loyal to two countries or even have sympathy with Iran. Additionally, you have to think about using anti-Iranian forces. You can thwart Iranian plans by using your influence inside Iran through organizations such as Mujahideen-e-Khalq or others.

You must work on creating major troubles inside Iran in a way that forces the Tehran regime to disperse its efforts in many directions. You want to create weaknesses, such as between different ethnic groups. For example, you can push the Arabs in Arabistan in a certain direction, since they are a large population, about 3 million to 4 million people, in an area that is easy for you to support, because it is close to you. These Arabs form a major problem for Iran on their side of the border.

The Kurds along the northern borders of Iraq are the other part of the process, where it is also possible to create problems. Another problem is the Baluchs on the eastern side of Iran. You can spread disaffection between the Baluchs in Afghanistan and those in Iran and try to deepen the current disagreement between both and the Iranians.

Woods: Since you brought up issue of the people of Arabistan, what was the nature of support for them by Saddam regime during the 8 years of the Iran-Iraq War?

Hamdani: They supported Iraq at the beginning, but one of the Iraqi commanders made a number of mistakes and the leadership did not care much about this part of the war. Tali Ad-Duri, the 9th Division commander, was an idiot and at the beginning of the war executed 58 people from Arabistan, simply because they did not want to deal with him. This was a turning point for support in Arabistan for the Iraqi army and Saddam's efforts to attract support. They have the same tribes that we have in southern Iraq, especially the Bani Lam tribe.

Woods: I don't understand—why were they executed?

Hamdani: This idiot Tali along with another officer had a Ba'athist mentality. They believed that since the people of Arabistan were Arabs, they must instantly obey Ba'ath orders and if they refused to, then they need to be executed. The people of Arabistan sympathized with us at the war's beginning. Ayatollah Khomeini had told them at the beginning of the revolution that they were brothers and promised to build new relations with them. However, he and his Iranian subordinates acted as dictators and as if they were his soldiers. At the beginning of the war, the people of Arabistan did not comply with Khomeini's orders, and he considered them traitors.

The people of Arabistan were also prepared to act on our behalf because they had been oppressed during the Shah's era. When Khomeini first came in power, he came in with a positive political framework and gave the impression he was there for all Iranian ethnic groups, which was wrong. They are now again oppressed, and they have little loyalty to the Iranian religious or political leaders.

So we start with this preliminary stage in Iraq, and then cross the border to cause trouble in Iran and only then move to military concepts.

One thing is sure. We should not consider the immediate military actions, such as sending large forces into Iran. Iran is a huge country. It is four times bigger than Iraq and requires large units with high-tech equipment and capabilities. Therefore, we should rely on military air and missile strikes to destroy their air bases and damage their economy to weaken them and drain support for their military industrial complex. So if we destroy their economic infrastructure in a few days, this should lead directly to their collapse.

Since their economic situation is weak, as it is right now, and most Iranian leaders tend to focus on the military-economic perspective, we should try to hit that area as fast as possible so that an attack will have a major impact on the overall morale and the economy of Iran as a whole.

In order for air and missile strikes to be successful, they require an accurate database. The strike has to be doubly strong. For example, we should send 10 aircraft per strike for each target so that the destruction will be effective enough not to give them the chance to rebuild.

Certainly, many of Iran's mobile missile bases will be able to execute their attacks. We must be prepared to bear missile attacks, unless we possess the capability to shoot down or destroy these missiles. The Iranians will definitely make a number of damaging attacks on certain vital areas of Iraq with missiles, such as Shahab–2 or Shahab–3, especially if they are mobile.

It is important to gauge the reaction of Iranian troops. . . . I received this information from the officers who went to Iran. They indicated that when one goes out on the street and interacts with the Iranian people, one realizes that the young generation is the real weakness of Iran's regime.

Murray: It also appears to be a generation that is revolting against its elders by seeking Western influences and Western attitudes.

Hamdani: I agree with you. This generation has started looking to the West lately and is launching a counterrevolution against the clerics.

Woods: These first couple of elements that you have talked about: securing your homeland, identifying the weak spots in the enemy population and then targeting critical infrastructure. In hindsight, were these viable options for Saddam in 1980?

Hamdani: Yes, but Saddam Hussein did not honor time. He did not notice the changing environment. You cannot face revolutionary elements like the Khomeini regime with limited tactics. Saddam's mistake was that he was always in a hurry.

This point about the Iranian youth is such an important point. I just want to go back and emphasize the importance and the impact of a new generation and how it is critical to the stability of Iran and the Iranian government as a whole. One of the Iraqi generals who visited Tehran in summer 2003 had a chance to talk to an

Iranian Revolutionary Guard officer while they were walking around in the streets of Tehran. The Iraqi officer noticed that Iranian youth have access to the Internet, the growing number of satellite dishes, and all that television stuff; he asked the Iranian Revolutionary Guard officer, "What's this? Is this something new?" The response was "This is our problem. . . . We are really not looking to provoke the new generation because, when we look back, we know it was the young generation that actually brought Khomeini and built the Revolutionary Guard." So in other words, the Iranian youth does not have much loyalty to the regime.

The other thing Iran lacked [according to the Revolutionary Guard officer] was an effective air force. Iran, with its large area, used to mobilize its troops by railroads and Iraq's air forces were unable to destroy the railroad centers, which caused us great difficulty.

Iraq would have to have smart weapons, so that it could take the risk of going deep inside Iran, and precision bombs. I mean the United States uses smart bombs and goes in without protection. Iraqi aircraft could only carry regular bombs, whose accuracy was poor.

The situation would have been different, had Iraq possessed smart weapons and benefited from satellite information. Satellites would have allowed us to launch followup strikes based on accurate battle damage assessments, so that the overall results would have had greater impact.

Then there is the terrain. There are Iranian gorges that are the primary access point for Iran's army. For instance, the Baitaq Gorge is critical (I always pictured defending there, when I was at the war college). If one laid out a defense plan against Iran that included the defense of the northern area of Iraq, one must control Baitaq Gorge. It is this gorge that allows large military convoys to proceed from the Iranian side. This is only one. At certain areas, but not all over all the Iranian territory, there are these gorges . . . passages that facilitate either the movement of light forces or the hitting and destroying of them.

In the Western areas of Iran, valleys define these areas, such as in the Zagros. You cannot move in the Zagros Mountains unless you move through a limited number of roads and valleys. The mistake we made in 1980 was that all Iraqi troops rushed 10–20 kilometers into Iran along the length of the border. We thought that the minute the Iraqi army went in, Bazergan, the leader of counter-Islamic revolutionary forces, would take over the government. What is the military use of going into Mehran or somewhere else? The right thing to have done would have been to define your effort and control the access points back to your strategic reserves—control the lines of communications. Instead, our military efforts were spread all over the border.

Our army was small and the possibility of our troops going to the appropriate sites in depth was slim in 1980. The maximum we could have moved inside

Iran was 10–20 kilometers from the border. Besides, we did not have a clear operational objective to reach. To succeed, the operational objective of the troops has to be defined. If we gathered our troops and controlled these critical areas, we would have held the Iranian reserves at a disadvantage and severely limited their options.

Murray: How effective was Iraqi air interdiction in terms of shutting off these access points?

Hamdani: We had aircraft, but there were not enough of them and we could not continue attacks day and night because of a shortage of aircraft. The lack of capability and training, especially operating at night, and the lack of night vision were a major factor. We just did not possess the capabilities at the time. Iraq's air forces did not reach an appropriate level until 1986.

Even after we created this air force, it was not sufficient. In June 1988, we pushed the MEK deep into Iran. Unfortunately, we could not provide them with the air support they required. The MEK pushed all the way down to Garamis, where they ran into 15 brigades of Iranian Pasdaran. We were able to support them with a few Sukhoi–22s during the day, but nothing at night. We could hear the MEK crying over the radio because their losses were so high and our aircraft were so few. So even in 1988, we did not possess all the capability needed to support troops operating deep inside Iran.

There are many places like this in Iran, where nothing but the high walls of mountains and narrow roads, where two cars can hardly get past each other. I often wondered, "What if we rushed in and occupied this location."[95] It is very steep. If at this location . . . we had crossed here and we crossed that one . . . we would have prevented many of our future problems. If only we controlled these mountains and blocked these gorges, it would have immensely bettered our situation by breaking Iran's army up into two halves. It is all gorges . . . big gorges. We need major engineering effort to destroy the passes. We could have destroyed them with bulldozers and explosives, had we reached them.

Murray: Iraq's combat engineers appear to have been excellent. Why did Iraq during the 8 years of war with Iran not use its combat engineers to close these gorges?

Hamdani: The problem was that we withdrew from all these areas in 1982. This mistake happened at the beginning of the war. Our working premise was that the minute our forces drove 10–20 kilometers into Iran, the regime in Tehran would collapse. We only thought about the potential success of this assumption, while in reality it was one of the worst plans.

In my memoirs, I mentioned three divisions during the initial invasion of Iran without once specifying the objective of their missions. This is because they were all fighting with the same objective in mind. Baghdad was just pushing everybody to the front. Although I was a relatively junior officer, even I could not ignore this issue. I mean this is war and there should be a specific mission for each unit. This is a basic instruction at the platoon and company level in the military academy, and obviously, it should apply all the way up to the level of the chief of staff. At the level of a platoon or an army, there must be a specific mission!

As for the southern sector of the Iran-Iraq border, almost the entire area is flat. However, the Iranians constructed a number of irrigation channels, through which they could direct the flow of water. They could direct the water in these irrigation channels in certain seasons, toward the dams or use it to destroy the bridges over the Karun River and that cross to the Karkha area.

If we go in depth regarding the southern sector, these areas are also confined. There are a limited number of strategic roads, enclosed in narrow valleys, which the Iranians could destroy as described earlier. If you block this area, you block the main rail line to Tehran. If you actually close this road network, you close virtually all contact between the south and the north and with it any Iranian logistic support.

Woods: So in this alternate history we are discussing, what areas would you identify as the Iraqi military objectives in the 1980 invasion?

Hamdani: The area into which we advanced is almost all open area, except for some small pieces of ground. We could have had armored forces reach the Al-Ahwaz area and easily the Hanin camp. We actually advanced most of the way, but we never closed these key north-south logistics routes. That was the first great mistake. Our armor just stopped in this location.

However, if we had possessed a strong air force with forward air bases, the minute Iranian troops advanced close to these areas we could have cut them off from their support. Remember, we did not have any reaction from the Iranians during the first 3 months of the war. We had full control until the Iranian strategic reserves arrived from the depths of their country. And the Iranian strategic reserves had to move through these narrow access points. It would have had a psychological impact from the soldier's perspective to be cut off from reinforcements and backup support. The Iranian defenders would know when you began targeting their logistic routes. Moreover, as I already mentioned, things would have been much easier if we had maintained good relations with the Arabs in Arabistan.

Woods: What do you think the Iranians learned from these 1980 experiences?

Hamdani: For sure, as far as the thinking and preparation level of their army, the Iranians have reached the level of sophistication of the Iraqi army in 1990. Their political economy dictates a deterrence strategy. This means they will maintain a big force. This is a security force, but in fact, as far as military education and strategy, they remain weak. Their strategy was weak in the 1980s, and therefore, they relied on young men. This youth is almost finished now. Based on their speeches and the way they talk, which is a lot like the Iraqis did in 1990 before Kuwait, the Iranians are constructing a facade. They want to be seen as a major power, as a kind of superpower in the region. Nevertheless, in reality, they have their weaknesses, and one of the weaknesses is actually the new generation. Most of the generation that fought and were loyal to Khomeini are now much older, and they really can no longer rely on the young generation to fill in. When it comes to protecting sensitive things, they know that, if the enemy has the technology, there is no point of putting a division-level force here to defend. This is especially true if they know—and they should—that their enemy will not come on the ground, but instead will destroy the sensitive targets with an air campaign.

Woods: Given the changes in the current Iranian generation, do you think the Iranian army or the Iranian leadership has significantly changed their operational approach and warfighting doctrine to compensate? Is one way to deal with the new generation to rely instead on armored forces, helicopters, and high technology, instead of the human-wave mentality of the previous war?

Hamdani: That is exactly why they rely on missiles and their air force at present. Iran uses its mobile missiles to act as a deterrence force. They rely on their missiles not as a destructive force, but as a deterrent force to discourage others from attacking them. This is even true of their air defense systems. Iran has thousands of vital targets but has an ineffective air defense system. It is a large country with thousands of targets. Iran wants to protect its command headquarters, its air bases, its factories, its nuclear project, its ports, its oil fields, as well as its military infrastructure, the roads, and bridges. The air defense forces of the old Soviet Union would not be enough for this task.

There are approximately 30,000 vital targets in Iran and each target requires one air defense battery at least. That is why Iran has focused on deterrence and that is why it is working on a nuclear project to reach a level of equivalence; this equivalence in deterrence will achieve the objective. The more Ahmadinejad screams, the more he expresses Iran's weakness. We, as Iraqis, went through a lot, but we do not express our suffering because to do so would represent weakness.

Murray: Why do you think the Iranians did not take advantage of Iraq's difficulties in 1991, 1992, or 1993?

Hamdani: They did. Their actions were a continuation of the war. But they were smart in this regard. The Iranians gained wisdom after 1988; they now believed that since Iraq was heading toward its end, the process was America's responsibility. Therefore, to encourage the United States to continue to the end of what became the invasion of 2003, Iran should not provoke another conflict and generate more problems. Moreover, if they were to make a move like that, once they crossed into Iraq and the red line border again, the Iraqi people would have unified against them. Iran did not want that. Iran knew the Iraqi-American confrontation was heading to an end. At the same time, they knew that as a result of the weaknesses created by the sanctions, the time was right for Iran to work inside Iraq's body.

There is another reason why they waited: the 8-year war had exhausted them. They reorganized their structure, and, through the Soviet Union [and Russia], obtained the weapons they needed.

Iran acted wisely. After the war ended, they coordinated their activity carefully. Even today the Iranian leadership acts with considerable wisdom in regard to many issues. Even the relations between the Iranian Ministry of Foreign Affairs, the Ministry of Defense, and the Pasdaran have improved significantly since 1990, when everyone acted as they wished. A symphony was born with a maestro who distributes the roles appropriately. The influence and force of religious leaders have weakened considerably throughout the years.

Discussion Fifteen

Armor Operations — Bravery and the Warrior Mentality — Saddam's Misunderstanding of Military Technology — Integration of Helicopter and Tank Capabilities — Lessons Learned on Artillery, Iraq, and Iran — Changes in Iranian Command and Control — Iranian Tactical and Operational Developments

Woods: What I would like to do is to cover some broad military areas and just ask for your thoughts on a range of military issues. Let us take armor operations, for example. Based on your experience, what has changed, what is changing, what is the future of armor operations in the Middle East?

Hamdani: In general, I think armed helicopters are now like the tank; they have started to take over from the tanks. For instance, the [AH–64] Apache aircraft changed many concepts of the use of armored troops.

One day, I had a meeting with Saddam Hussein and he asked me to explain the changes that had occurred, and how to deal with the American Army. What are the existing difficulties? I used a piece of paper to draw out the answer, since Saddam was not a military person. There was an Iraqi T–72 tank [General draws a tank] and then there was an [American M–1] Abrams tank. So these are advanced systems. But one tank is not a substitute for the other. I gave the T–72 a value of 1.5 out of 5, while the M–1 gets a 5 out of 5. Both tanks fire the sabot rounds with muzzle velocities of 1,800 meters per second. The ultimate range of the T–72 for a first-round hit is 2,200 meters, while the Abrams tank can produce a first-round hit at 3,000 meters.

In addition [drawing a helicopter over the M–1 tank], we can see the Apache helicopter which carries the Hellfire missile [hovering] above the Abrams.

Each [helicopter] carries 16 of these missiles, and the Hellfire has a range of 8,000 meters. This type of missile has a 90 percent probability of hitting its target.

Above this Apache, you have an A–10 [Thunderbolt II ground attack jet]. This aircraft also carries missiles with extended ranges. Then, there are F–16 aircraft and the F–15 above that. Above that are the Blackbird, the reconnaissance information aircraft and above that, are the U–2, the AWACS [airborne warning and control system], and satellite systems. All this for one mission! That mission is to detect the tank location and its maneuver area. However, the T–72 has no aerial cover. So that on our quality scale, the U.S. tank with a 5 might become a 25. Because of a lack of support, the T–72 with a value of 1.5 may become -5.

This is what I explained to Saddam. What does the tank require? It requires firepower, self-protection, and maneuverability. As a result of being detected in real time, all weapons are going to range in on it. This tank is not going to be able to detect the enemy weapons aiming at it, because the maximum range of T–72 observation is 5,000 meters, while the Apache has an 8,000-meter range. So there is a 3,000-meter difference, where one can watch, the other one is blind. The T–72 cannot maneuver because of the satellite detection or the Blackbird reconnaissance and the new unmanned aircraft. Even these unmanned aircraft carry missiles that the Americans can guide. So this tank becomes nothing.

I went on to explain to Saddam that there is no point to having all this armor, if they cannot maneuver or move.

Woods: How did Saddam respond to your explanation?

Hamdani: He was shocked. He was shocked and disappointed. He told me, "You always talk to me with numbers. But you say 1 plus 1 equals 2, while for me 1 might be equal to 10." He said, "You are a good commander at the technical level, but bad at the morale level."

All this means is that the tank is worthless in Iraq and the Middle East without having the support of the air force, radar, and detection equipment.

Murray: It seems to me that Saddam's answer would always be that it would be the Iraqi soldier, by his own bravery as a warrior, who would make all that technology worthless.

Hamdani: True . . . true. As I mentioned earlier, just before the 1991 war, when I told the Republican Guard staff that the American plan was going to be along the Wadi al-Batin and that what we were doing was wrong, they became furious with me. They said that I was demoralizing the subordinate officers, that I had upset the president, and that I was going to be referred to a court-martial. The reason for this was that these senior staff had reached a point where they degraded our intelligence. For instance, Hussein Kamel would say, "The Abrams tank is heavy; the minute it moves in the sand it will sink! As for the F–15 or F–16 aircraft, when we fire a flare gun at them at night, the pilot will blink and lose control of the aircraft." Saddam Hussein would say, "Throw sand on the Phantom and that is it." This discussion happened on November 23, 1990.[96]

Woods: Did the Iranians learn lessons from watching these operations in 1991? Are these rather simplistic conceptions of modern war what you would expect from the Iranians?

Hamdani: They learned for sure, but the problem is they have the same mentality. The problem of the leadership mentality in much of the Middle East is that it looks at people as a herd of sheep or animals. Middle Eastern leaders do not want anyone beside themselves to think, whether one talks about Iran, or Iraq, or the entire Middle East.

The current Iranian forces possess the T–72 tanks, as well as old tanks such as T–55 and T–62, and they maneuver with their air force. But I notice that they always rely on the infantry, which the tanks support. This indicates that they still possess the old assumptions. The second thing is that whoever does not possess helicopters, like the Apache or the Russian Hind Mi-24 helicopter, or is unable to use them in a coordinated way, and who does not possess reasonable air superiority, has useless hulks of metal in tanks. You are fighting an army. Yes, Iran may fight an army from the Middle East, but it will find it hard to fight an army like the American army, because it is hard to have a balance or be equal to the American army, except in a nontraditional war.

Woods: That brings up the question about how Iran used its AH–1 attack helicopters during the Iran-Iraq War. Did you see evidence in the 1980s that Iran was attempting that, and do you think that they started to integrate their tank and helicopter capabilities?

Hamdani: They tried to use it the same way. The Cobra is an American aircraft, and it was paired with Russian T–55s.

The Russian helicopter [Hind] could not hover in a firing position, so it kept circling. The Gazelle, Apache, and Cobra helicopters can take a hover position. The hover position works best. Let us say there is a hill, the helicopter comes up like a tank that gets behind the hill and launches its missile.

The Iranians did use the Cobra well and achieved great results as far as attacking armor while we used the Gazelle and Mi-24. But this equipment is of an older generation compared with the Apache. The Apache can have up to 16 missiles, while the older aircraft hold only 3 or 4. In 1991, I watched as an Apache destroyed a complete armored brigade, right before my eyes, in 15 minutes.

Mechanized troops in the Middle East will not have any value against an international force like the United States, if they cannot gain air superiority, even locally. Local forces will be able to balance each other only when facing other local forces.

In June of 2002, 1997, and 1995, I presented studies regarding this matter. I talked with Saddam in this regard and told him, "Every one of the previous corps is worthless because any armor without air protection is useless."

In 1992, I presented a study on the 1991 war. This study presented lessons stating that catching up with the technology of the American army is such an impossible process and therefore, we should turn to the guerrilla war. Saddam did not listen. He spent 60 percent of the national income on military industrialization to catch up with the American technology, which was obviously an unsuccessful project.

Woods: What lessons emerged from the Iran-Iraq War in terms of artillery operations and what, if any, future trends do you see in artillery operations in general?

Hamdani: Artillery development had three aspects: first, the area coverage that relies on land survey, the distance, direction, and so forth represents the base for artillery action and developed as a result of computers.

They will look for a tactical point, a physical point on the ground and the map, and then the reconnaissance group will measure the area and distance. This information will be useful for artillery opening and identifying its targets. At the present, computers and satellites do this.

Self-propelled artillery is similar to the tank. The movement of such artillery is not limited; you can open it easily anywhere. But it has the same vulnerability as the tank, if there is no air protection.

The other development in artillery is missile guidance. Artillery currently, for instance, the American army, the Israeli army, and the French army, launches guided missiles. Even mortars are now easy to guide with a laser.

The other development lies in radars capable of tracking the enemy's artillery. This development, whether it was in Iran or previously in Iraq, remained limited. Both sides still relied on the mobile artillery and regular missiles, developed with regard for area usage. For instance, there is a British calculator that computes 30 targets at a time. We have a book that has firing schedules for the type of missile, the amount of charge, temperature, pressure, and humidity.

This was one of the firing tables that listed the target and math calculations. But now we have computers that store the data. Each company had this in the early 1980s, with 300 targets. This facilitated artillery opening and firing on the targets.

Woods: With regard to Iranian artillery, what would you say was the biggest difference between the capabilities of the 1980s compared with developments after 1990?

Hamdani: After it, they received Russian weapons at cheap prices, as well as Russian trainers. When the Soviet Union collapsed in 1989–1990, the Iranians even started to look for possible nuclear weapons. There were more than 15 Iranian business groups based in former Soviet areas trying to buy all kinds of different weapons. They bought weapons such as different aircraft, armor, and artillery. They also discussed with North Korea the issue of technology for manufacturing missiles. Pakistan was the mediator in these talks. Then, there were the 135 Iraqi aircraft flown to Iran during the 1991 war and not returned. These included Sukhoi-27, which is an advanced aircraft. Iran trained with them and bought spare parts. After 1991, the Iranians started to develop these aircraft.

But the problem, as before, was their mentality. The existing Iranian high command remained traditional, especially when it came to religious loyalty, and the religious scholars continued to affect the way the soldiers could execute their plans and operations.

As far as artillery, they focused on missile launchers, such as the Grad [BM–21] and other similar launchers. They wanted to achieve high fire density with maximum speed, so that they could move and change locations.

Overall, they tried to expand their industrial base, since they knew that some day they might confront the opposition that Iraq had met. Therefore, they manufactured the majority of their requirement for munitions, mortars, medium range machineguns, and tank parts themselves. They focused on developing an industrial base, which was the right thing to do.

After 1991, they did not consider Iraq a threat anymore. Therefore, they focused on coastal weapons, airborne forces, and missiles: weapons like the Chinese missile C–4, coastal artillery and mines, which can be laid and remotely guided. They also started to manufacture small boats, torpedo boats.

Since they were not going to rely on armor, they decided to fight the Americans along the Gulf. In addition, they worried about how to protect critical areas of Iran. They thought about how to launch counterattacks using airborne forces, including heliborne forces. But as I have already stated, what I noticed in their televised training maneuvers was that they still rely on parachuting, which requires air superiority.

In Iran's review of the recent war, they focused on how to maintain their C^2. The C^2 system for Iran is, of course, a major system similar to the C^4I [command, control, communications, computers, and information] system Americans have.[97] They also focused on radar and air defense systems in particular. Fifty percent of Iran's efforts goes into air defense, since they expect American air attack.

But regardless of the weapons, the Iranian army's biggest issue will remain the education of its soldiers, the education of its officers, and the education of its commanders. They remain loyal to the methods of Third World countries.

Woods: You mentioned C^2. How much do you think Iranian battlefield C^2 has changed since the Iran-Iraq War?

Hamdani: In fact, the Iranians did realize that their behavior during the war with Iraq, where each party worked in a way that destroyed the overall effort, was wrong. At the present, they have everyone under one system, even the army. I have heard they are considering establishing an advanced C^2 system, where they can focus on air defense as well as coordinate among all the Iranian forces, whether ground force, air, or naval.

This idea of creating a new C^2 center to coordinate among all the forces is a positive thing. But it also makes the center a sensitive target, because once you destroy it, it will take the Iranians time and effort to rebuild it, and they will have to go back to old fashioned ways of C^2.

Woods: In other areas of military operations, you noted that the Iranians had not changed tactics since the 1980s. Why do you think that is the case?

Hamdani: It was not easy for the Iranians, since they could imagine another war with Iraq like the last one. They thought Iraq was no longer capable of representing a conventional threat to them. But just in case, they have established red lines they believe cannot be crossed openly, and therefore they have turned their military doctrine into a doctrine of interference in the internal affairs of Iraq by using ambiguous tools. For instance, they have relied on intelligence operatives. You have Iranian intelligence in charge of the Mahdi army, the Pasdaran in charge of the higher council, and the Islamic courts in charge of Ad-Da'wa party.

Iranian intelligence will coordinate secret channels with the Mahdi army. You have the Revolutionary Guards instruct, organize, and arm the Badr groups, which is now the Iraqi Ministry of Interior. Islamic Courts support through secret channels the Ad-Da'wa party, while the intelligence section of the Iranian Ministry of Defense directs other portions of that body. So their action does not aim at the direct use of armies, but the use of influence by connecting secret channels through direct support and armament. At the same time, they provide these groups with training camps for their agents in Iraq, whether for the Mahdi army, Badr, or others at the officers level. At the same time, they have training camps for Hizballah: the Iraqi Hizballah, the Iranian Hizballah, and the Lebanese—all together. Therefore, you find most of the people involved speak Arabic, but with a Lebanese dialect, because they relied basically on Hizballah training camps in Lebanon and Iran.

So the conventional military doctrine supports Iran with regular forces that defend the nation. The underground military consists of supporting the forces loyal to Iran abroad and relies on regular forces for support, for instance, Hizballah or Hamas. They have used Hamas, Islamic Jihad, and Hizballah (through Nasrallah). These are all secret channels; all this armament, equipment, and supply—32,000 militia members in Iraq get their salaries from Iran. So if we wanted to focus on just the military, the Iranian army we see, as far as the ground forces, air force and navy force, are only involved in defending Iran. The offensive and infiltration forces of Iran take place through unseen tools.

Discussion Sixteen

Recommendations for U.S. Actions in Iraq from May 2007

Woods: General, I would like to hear your recommendations about what actions the United States should take, that are realistically available, with regard to Iraq. Please include any comments you wish on issues of politics, governance, military, and security. Let us look ahead, moving forward from today in May 2007.

Hamdani: Well, looking at the current situation in Iraq, it appears as though there is no security. Thus, there is no easy solution, but in fact, if we familiarize ourselves with the origin of the problems, the solution makes itself more apparent. So let me take us in that direction to investigate the origin of these problems and thus better understand what we need to do today.

The current security issue in Iraq derives from a political problem that resulted from an incorrect understanding of the political situation by the Americans who developed policy for Iraq. The foundation of the American project rested on the incorrect facts and information supplied by opposition parties. Instead of resolving the problem of Saddam Hussein, that process created other problems linked tightly to regional problems, especially with the issue of Iran. Iran benefited enormously from the American investment in eliminating Saddam's regime, while being able to turn the Iraqi position against the United States. Iran was simply not interested in helping the representatives of American forces and American authority in Iraq, but rather manipulated American capabilities to act on behalf of Iranian strategy.

The mistakes [Paul] Bremer made resulted from the belief that there are Shia, Kurds, and Sunnis, and the former regime was a part of the Arab Sunni group. But this is not true. The former regime was led by an Iraqi leader who did not subscribe to this division.

The American political project intended to eliminate Saddam Hussein and his group and transition from a dictatorial authoritarian regime to a democratic system in a single phase. But American leaders misunderstood the fact that Iraq would require a transitional phase between dictatorship and democracy, which would have looked like an autocratic system. American planners should have recognized that if their forces were successful in occupying Iraq and overthrowing Saddam's regime, it would be necessary to keep the Iraqi forces, the army, the security forces, as well as the state's fundamental governmental institutions, in place while changing key leaders with second-line leaders for the purposes of administering the state through a transitional phase. Then, the American authority could have dealt with service matters in Iraq to demonstrate that it was not just an occupying force. It could have presented itself as aiming to compensate Iraq for the long period of time when Saddam had wasted its human, financial, and spiritual resources. So if there were an American governor acting as a higher authority, but with the same government and institutions, especially the security forces, then electrical, water, health, educational, and other services would have continued, and all of this would have provided the Iraqi citizens with a good impression about Iraq's future and the American project.

The political development process would have required that any internal conflicts and different interests that were a part of the numerous conflicts be repressed for a time, so that the American authority could carry out a gradual transition process to democracy, beginning with open diplomatic relations and the sending of delegations to the United States, Britain, and other European countries, to return with American and European aid to build democratic institutions. Democracy is based on history and heritage. One cannot achieve it by pressure or by opening and shutting buttons. It requires a transitional period of no less than 5 to 10 years in order for the democratic institutions to rest on an acceptable educational and cultural level to gain people's acceptance. At the same time, those who experienced this comprehensive regime change would feel that they had a role in the governance so that they could begin practicing democratic life from the lowest through the highest levels.

The problem with the American project is that it was the destruction of a country using "the bulldozer method," which was difficult, and exacerbated the processes for rebuilding as well.

We have to compare ourselves with the British regime in 1920. The Brits built a state on the ruins of the Ottoman empire. They brought out the best in the Iraqi people. The real builders came from British expertise, so that they established a state in a short period.

The problem with the American project was that it was a plan for the destruction of a country. But the destruction process does not need competence; destruction is easier than building and does not require technique. Not everyone who went to the United States and Europe opposing the politics of Saddam Hussein was a politician. But we have to reach the next phase, where we look for true Iraqi builders at any level. The key condition must be their loyalty to Iraq.

So the United States rushed in establishing the state's regime and a new constitution. This became the biggest problem because it involved the allocation issue, and gave the forces controlled by Iran the chance to establish themselves. They did, and then tried to defend what they acquired. Similarly, the Kurdish political parties in the north established themselves and tried to defend their acquisitions at the expense of others, including the issues of Kirkuk and Mosul.

Each of the Shia parties started to work for its own interests and then, with the emerging issue of illegal investments of the national government's resources, and especially the oil issue and the new mafia issue (each mafia having its own armed force), these parties formed militias to protect themselves from the forces of their opponents.

If we return to the issue of the Iraqi army, one cannot consider the current army as a national army, because it was not built on the basis and organizational principles of the armed forces of any country. That basis must rest on three main principles: one, the national political goal; two, the union of the leadership; and three, transfer of authority from a professionally determined institution of standards.

What happened as a result of Bremer's resolutions was the legalization of the militias. The Peshmerga became an army and Bedouins entered certain forces. At the same time, the other wing of the Da'wa party established the Ministry of National Security. As a result, this became a military force serving the centers of force, rather than a hierarchical state. The current prime minister, Al-Maliki, for example, does not deserve the title of prime minister, but rather the head of a ministry, because he has no control or command to run a broad-based approach in his ministry.

Therefore, the correct way to reform the current situation, though this is a tough choice, but the right one, is to use the new strategy of multiplying the American forces, especially in Baghdad. If the American forces take over the security role, especially in Baghdad, and control Baghdad and Iraq entirely, then this process of taking over the role of security means the elimination and/or reduction of the power of the militias. This could lead to the establishment of a national political regime of technocrats loyal to Iraq, who will work under American supervision and with American help, but who remain loyal to Iraq, and not under Iranian influence or any other group.

Another problem I would like to mention is Iran. Even the criminal gangs, bandits, and others have all started to defend themselves. So if there is no force multiplication to start with, for the security directorate or to establish a government and then rebuild the Iraqi national armed forces loyal to Iraq, the Iraqi flag, and the head of state, then we cannot respond. But where is the problem? The current armed forces have a poorly designed constitutional organization under the prime minister as the general commander of the armed forces. But the prime minister represents a party and has a militia. And if we link it to the president and the current president, he will remain the head of a party and the head of a militia. There were never independent national forces. The independent forces should connect to a higher figure who represents the country's sovereignty. Therefore, we should aim at defining the general position of the armed forces as independent, with a key organization to rebuild the armed forces. The president should be independent as well, in order to become the commander of the armed forces, or rather the general commander of the armed forces. In this case, the Ministry of Defense, the Chief of Staff of the Army, and the Ministry of the Interior, and a military cadre of independent and professional officers who work according to a professional system with professional standards, within 6 months to 1 year would be able to establish national forces able to assume the security responsibilities inside the country and fight existing terrorist force or forces.

So on the one hand, we would be able to deal with the current problem in the Iraqi army and the Ministry of the Interior with positive methods. On the other hand, we need to establish an economic program that enables small projects on the family level, to decrease the need to carry weapons. This is a set of solutions that could underpin a true national project to build a unified Iraq, and an Iraq that relies on a national force that serves the state and does not serve any other country or interest.

Endnotes

[1] The Iraqi Perspectives Project (IPP) is an Institute for Defense Analyses (IDA) research effort sponsored by U.S. Joint Forces Command. The IPP, begun in 2003, combined oral histories and archival research to understand the Iraqi side of recent military operations.

[2] For a brief description of the nature and impact of the post–World War II projects similar to Project 1946, see Kevin Soutor, "To Stem the Red Tide: The German Report series and its Effects on American Defense Doctrine, 1948–1954," *Journal of Military History* (October 1993).

[3] General Hamdani recently published his memoirs, *Before History Left Us* (Beirut: Arab Scientific Publishers, 2006). Author references to Hamdani's memoirs refer to an unpublished translation of an earlier draft manuscript of the published memoir.

[4] The interviews were conducted in Arabic and English via a translator. The interviews were also recorded and later transcribed to enhance the translator's words. American colloquialisms in Hamdani's responses may be the result of the translator's and the interviewers' desire for clarity over strictly literal translation.

[5] The 1973 Arab-Israeli War was fought from October 6 to October 26, 1973. Israel faced an Arab coalition led by Egypt and Syria. This was is also known as the Yom Kippur War, the Ramadan War, the October War, and the Fourth Arab-Israeli War.

[6] This theme will be explored in a future IDA study in the IPP series focusing on the Iran-Iraq War.

[7] General Haig, British Expeditionary Force commander in World War I, has, to some degree, come to symbolize a cavalier, uninformed, and criminally naive command view of casualties of that war. During the Battle of the Somme in July 1916, Haig recorded in his diaries how he was "not perturbed" by the 165,000 British casualties incurred at that point. After all, he noted, the losses "were only about one hundred and twenty thousand more than they would have been had we not attacked." Robert Pois and Philip Langer, *Command Failure in War: Psychology and Leadership* (Bloomington: Indiana University Press, 2004), 131.

[8] General Hamdani was a major (armor officer) at the beginning of the war.

[9] Throughout the interview, General Hamdani exhibited a general suspicion of Iran's motives and especially of the Shia political organizations of Iraq, which he tended to conflate as simply puppets of Iran, incapable of acting independently. This view extended throughout his discussions with us whether we were talking about the past or the present.

[10] Khorramshahr (also known as *Mohammerah* in Arabic) is a port city 10 kilometers north of Abadan at the confluence of the Arvand and Karun Rivers.

[11] Between January 1981 and June 1982, Iranian offenses at Susangard, Qasr-e-Shirin, and Dehloran generated horrendous casualties on both sides. In September 1981, Iran broke the siege of Abadan and a month later recaptured Bostan. In early 1982, Iraqi forces were driven back from gains on the northern front, and in May, Iran liberated Khorramshahr.

[12] A fact that makes the general suspicions and distrust of the Shia voiced by Hamdani all the more interesting, considering the present Sunni-Shia divide in Iraq.

[13] The Iranians were never able to gain any popular support among Iraq's Arab Shia community. They did, however, successfully establish underground political networks and expatriate groups opposed to the Ba'ath regime.

[14] This betrayal may in part explain Saddam's willingness to use chemical weapons against the Kurds in succeeding years.

[15] The fact that the international community made virtually no protest against the use of chemical weapons by the Iraqis underlines how much of a pariah state Iran had become by the mid-1980s. Throughout the interviews, General Hamdani seemed to view the use of chemical weapons as an inevitable progression of the conflict and their effects less than extraordinary.

[16] Something similar was to occur during the course of the Iraq war in 2003, so that Saddam and his cronies remained optimistic right up to the last moment.

[17] Throughout our discussions, General Hamdani mentioned several times the pernicious effect of the Tikriti mafia. From the time of the 1968 Ba'ath revolution, men from Tikrit came to dominate the ranks of state leadership and positions in the military.

[18] General Hamdani termed the C^2 on both sides throughout the war as "chaos"—a reflection undoubtedly of the educational weaknesses in both Iranian and Iraqi societies as well as the lack of technological sophistication.

[19] In Hamdani's comments on the Shia-Iranian connection, it can be difficult to distinguish between Arab Sunni nationalist positions and rational analyses of military affairs. This demographic shift had little to do with State encroachment. As Hamdani pointed out, the Shia population in Iraq during the mid-19th century was barely 10 percent of the total. By the 1920s, it had risen to 45 percent, and was now at 60 percent.

[20] The access that the seizure of Kuwait would have provided his navy may well have played a role in Saddam's thinking.

[21] During the latter part of the conflict, the Iranians and the Iraqis had fired hundreds of Scud missiles and modified Scuds at each other. The military and economic damage was minimal. Civilian casualties were heavy on both sides.

[22] Our earlier work on Saddam and the 2003 war with the United States indicates that he and his henchmen were much more worried about the possibility of another Shia uprising like that of 1991 than of a major invasion of Iraq by U.S. military forces. Kevin M. Woods et al., *The Iraqi Perspectives Report: Saddam's Senior Leadership on Operation* Iraqi Freedom (Annapolis, MD: Naval Institute Press, 2006).

[23] Nassir resigned as president but then was returned to power after massive demonstrations.

[24] Abd Al-Rahman Arif (b. 1916) was president of Iraq from April 16, 1966, to July 16, 1968. Arif was the head of the Iraqi army following the 1963 coup that installed his brother as Iraqi's president. He was appointed president after his brother was killed in a helicopter crash. After the Ba'ath coup of 1968, Arif was exiled to Turkey.

[25] The Camp David Agreement (formally known as the Camp David Accords) was a U.S.-brokered agreement between Egyptian President Anwar Sadat and Israeli Prime Minister Menachem Begin. The accords, signed on September 17, 1978, led directly to the Israel-Egypt Peace Treaty, signed in Washington, DC, on March 26, 1979.

[26] Saddam Hussein staged a palace coup on July 16, 1979, by forcing long-time president al-Baker to resign and purging potential rivals. Tensions with Iran (a perennial issue) rose with the overthrow of the Shah of Iran in February 1979. Border clashes between Iraq and Iran began almost immediately, growing to full-scale war in September 1979.

[27] General Abd Al-Hakim Amer (December 11, 1919–September 14, 1967) quickly rose to prominence as a junior officer after participating in the military coup that overthrew King Farouk in 1952. He soon became Egypt's senior military officer and Nassir's vice-president. After Egypt's loss in the 1967 war, Amer was jailed and offered an "honorable" death by poison—which he accepted.

[28] General Sa'd al-Din el-Shathili (also transliterated as Saad El Shazly) was Egypt's chief of staff during the 1973 Arab-Israeli War.

[29] In March 1975, Iran and Iraq signed the Algiers Agreement and pledged noninterference in each others' internal affairs, which temporarily relieved tensions over the waterway.

[30] The Da'wa party (also known as the Islamic Da'wa party) was formed in the late 1950s. The Da'wa party resisted the Ba'ath secular agenda as well as the Sunni domination of Iraqi political affairs. In 1979, the party began to receive significant support from the revolutionary regime in Iran. Membership in the Da'wa party under Saddam was punishable by death.

[31] Ibrahim Al-Ja'afari (born Ibrahim al-Ashaiqir in 1947) was a long-time Da'wa party activist. In 1980, he fled to Iran and worked during the Iran-Iraq War through the antiregime group Supreme Council for the Islamic Revolution in Iraq. In 2003, Al-Ja'afari became a prominent member of the early post-Saddam governments under the United Iraqi Alliance coalition of parties.

[32] Mehdi Bazargan (1907–1995) was appointed prime minister of Iran on February 5, 1979, by the Ayatollah Khomeini after the Shah fled Tehran. Although he supported the revolution, he soon broke with the new regime because of his emphasis on liberal and democratic ideals over theological ones.

[33] Abu Ghraib is a town located 20 miles west of Baghdad.

[34] Including an assassination attempt against Tariq Aziz.

[35] Iraq possessed approximately 12 of the Soviet manufactured Tupolev Tu-22 (North Atlantic Treaty Organization–designated BLINDER) supersonic bombers in 1980. By 1988, six had been lost in combat with Iran.

[36] *Rasit* is a French-made ground surveillance radar.

[37] General Hamdani's use of the word *strategic* in this context aligns most closely with the U.S. military's definition of *operational*: "The level of war at which campaigns and major operations are planned, conducted, and sustained to achieve strategic objectives within theaters or other operational areas. Activities at this level link tactics and strategy by establishing operational objectives needed to achieve the strategic objectives, sequencing events to achieve the operational objectives, initiating actions, and applying resources to bring about and sustain these events." U.S. Department of Defense, Joint Publication 1–02, *Department of Defense Dictionary of Military and Associated Terms 12 April 2001* (as amended through 12 July 2007), available at <www.dtic.mil/doctrine/jel/doddict/>.

[38] In other parts of this interview and in his memoirs, Hamdani notes this concern was more prominent after setbacks in Iraq's operations.

[39] General Hamdani also mentions General Taher Mahmoud Shukri and General Muhammad Fatthi Amin as professional military advisors.

[40] General Hamdani was not a Tikriti as were many of his survivors and a large percentage of the Iraqi Ba'ath leadership.

[41] The Italians' mines were descendants of the "bouncing betty" antipersonnel mines the Germans had in World War II.

[42] Known as *Muhammarah* to the Iraqis.

[43] The Mujahideen-e-Khalq is an Islamic socialist organization founded in the mid-1960s in opposition to the Shah of Iran. The group initially supported and joined the revolution in 1979 but quickly fell out of favor and began a violent resistance campaign including coordinated military operations from safe havens in Iraq.

[44] This attack occurred in Tehran on June 28, 1981. According to one report, in addition to Ayatollah Beheshti, the attack killed 74 people including 14 ministers and 27 Majlis deputies. A similar attack on August 30 on Iran's National Security Council killed the new president Ali Rajai and his prime minister, Mohammad Javad Bahonar. Edgar O'Ballance, *The Gulf War* (London: Brassey's Defense Publishers, 1988), 66.

[45] Mehdi Bazargan was appointed prime minister on February 5, 1979, by Ayatollah Khomeini. He resigned from his post as prime minister (along with the rest of his cabinet) directly after the American hostage crisis, but then participated in the Iranian parliament. He wanted Iran to be an "Islamic Democratic Republic," not the Islamic Republic that Khomeini's revolution installed. He died of a heart attack in 1995.

[46] Sadegh Ghotbzadeh resigned as foreign minister in August 1980 in the heat of the American hostage crisis; he was arrested and executed in September 1982.

[47] The general draws on the maps provided to indicate the river's course, the minefields, and the areas of operation of the III and IV Corps.

[48] See figure 5 for map.

[49] The "volunteer" status may to some limited degree account for Pakistani support, but it is highly unlikely that "volunteers" from North Korea were not government-sanctioned.

[50] There was heavy use of chemical weapons by Iraq in April 1987 during Iran's Karbala VII Campaign in and around Basra.

[51] Hamdani commanded the 2^d Republican Guard Corps in 2003. By both reputation and position, he was one of the most important commanders in Iraq at this time, yet he thought it possible that Iraq may employ chemicals weapons during Operation *Iraqi Freedom*.

[52] Hamdani was referring to the map in figure 4 during this part of the discussion.

[53] The consensus figure for Kurdish casualties attributed to the Halabjah attacks in February-March 1988 is approximately 5,000.

[54] U.S. Secretary of State Colin L. Powell, "Remarks to the United Nations Security Council," for example Slide 25, New York City, February 5, 2003.

[55] See U.S. Government White Paper, "Iraqi Weapons of Mass Destruction Programs," February 13, 1998.

[56] In fact, the evidence in the Saddam tapes indicates that the Iraqis carried out small tests with chemical weapons (not very successful) in 1983 and then used these weapons extensively in one of the battles in 1984. Here Hamdani is not necessarily lying. As a battalion commander at this time, he may well have not known about the use of such weapons.

[57] The central sector of the southern theater comprised the Iraqi III and VI Corps.

[58] Wafiq al-Samarrai rose to lead the General Military Intelligence Directorate following the 1991 Gulf War. He defected in December 1994 and worked to overthrow Saddam Hussein. He is currently an advisor to Iraqi President Jalal Talabani.

[59] General Hamdani was mistaken. General al-Samarra'i defected in 1994.

[60] At the time of these interviews (May 2007), the Iraqi High Tribunal was completing the trial of seven defendants accused of crimes against humanity for actions against the Kurdish population during the 1987–1988 Anfal campaign. In June 2007, the trial resulted in death sentences for three of the defendants: Ali Hasan Majid (former secretary-general of the Ba'ath party's northern bureau), Sultan Hashem Ahmed al-Ta'i (former commander of I Corps and later Minister of Defense), and Hussein Rashid Al-Tikriti (former deputy for operational affairs to the chief of staff of the Iraqi army).

[61] The first two are German generals Heinz Guderian and Erwin Rommel, and the third is American general George Patton, all practitioners of armored warfare in World War II.

[62] Hamdani appears to be recalling the Churchill quote, "Battles are won by slaughter and maneuver. The greater the general, the more he contributes in maneuver, the less he demands in slaughter."

[63] Ayatollah Khamenei was the president of Iran from 1981 to 1989.

[64] Hussein Kamel (Hassan al-Majid) went on to become the director of the Military Industrial Commission. In this role he was responsible for Iraq's weapons of mass destruction and major weapons programs. Kamel defected to Jordan in August 1995. In February 1996, after being offered immunity, Kamel returned to Iraq and was killed.

[65] This position is the equivalent to the assistant chief of staff in a U.S. division.

[66] The location General Hamdani refers to is unclear.

[67] In response to a followup question about the relationship between this officer and the Republican Guard's final commander, Sayf-al-Din Al-Rawi, the general replied that while they were from the same family, they were not the same kind of men or generals. Hamdani added that there was a huge difference between the characters of these men.

[68] The Ra'd missiles are a family of missiles manufactured in Iran and based on the Soviet AT–3B Sagger antitank guided missile with a range of a few kilometers, although some sources refer to it as a copy of a Chinese or North Korean cruise missile (also Ra'd).

[69] During Operation *Iraqi Freedom*, General Hamdani's II Republican Guard Corps included the Baghdad Infantry Division. The Baghdad division was able to conduct a relief-in-place with the regular army's 34th Division at al-Kut just prior to the arrival and capture of the city by the forces of the Coalition's I Marine Expeditionary Force.

[70] The Soviet term *correlation of forces* is a much more complex idea than the Western concept of *balance of power* that tends to emphasize the military factor. A correlation of forces is simultaneously a quantitative and qualitative assessment. It includes military, political, economic, social, and moral factors, and the relative strength of alliances.

[71] General Hamdani mentions that this is the same building where Saddam Hussein was executed by the Iraqi government on December 30, 2006.

[72] The General was probably referring to the Bell 214ST helicopter. In 1985, the United States sold Iraq 31 of these helicopters for civilian use.

[73] Hamdani unpublished manuscript.

[74] Revolutionary Command Council member Mizban Khadr Hadi was assigned command of the so-called Central Euphrates region during Operation *Iraqi Freedom* in 2003.

[75] Kevin M. Woods et al., *The Iraqi Perspectives Report: Saddam's Senior Leadership on Operation* Iraqi Freedom (Annapolis, MD: Naval Institute Press, 2006).

[76] Late in the 1973 war, the United States rushed television-camera guided Maverick missiles to Israel. According to some sources, the Israelis' were able to destroy up to 50 Arab tanks with this new weapon. See Lon O. Nordeen, Jr., *Air Warfare in the Missile Age* (Washington, DC: Smithsonian Institution, 1985), 168.

[77] General Hamdani was a tank company commander during the 1973 Arab-Israeli War.

[78] Iraqi engineers had rigged the bridge in question for demolition but failed to accomplish the task. Combat engineers from the U.S. Army's 3d Infantry Division were able to clear the demolitions and keep the bridge intact. See Gregory Fontenot, E.J. Degen, and David Tohn, *On Point: The United States Army in Operation* Iraqi Freedom (Annapolis, MD: Naval Institute Press, 2005), 288–299.

[79] The Safavid dynasty (~1501–1722) ruled over an area that included all of modern Iran, most of modern Iraq, and eastern Turkey, and stretched to modern Pakistan to the east.

[80] The Sassanian Dynasty (~379–651) covered all of what is today modern Iran, extending west to the Black Sea and east to modern India.

[81] In 1538, Khayr ad-Din defeated the navy of Charles V (the Habsburg emperor of Spain) at the battle of Préveza.

[82] This is in reference to the Umayyad caliphate dynasty (~660–750) that ruled during the great expansion of early Islam. This is also used as a historical and religious basis for Sunni-dominated pan-Arab movements.

[83] This representation of the Shia articles of faith may reflect the general's own Sunni background, as his account does not match the dominant orthodox view of Twelver Shi'ism, the tradition currently in power in Iran.

[84] The overall negotiations (between the Ottoman "Young Turks" and the Persians) were known as the Constantinople Protocols of 1913. The specific issue of the Shatt al-Arab was agreed to in a subordinate agreement known as the Protocol of Teheran that was written as an annex to the existing 1947 Ard Roum II Treaty.

[85] Officially known as the Treaty of the Iran-Iraq Frontier, it generally confirmed the 1913 agreement and added language to explicitly recognize international (primarily British) interests in the new and growing oil concessions in the region.

[86] Rezah Shah ruled Iran from 1925 until his abdication following the Anglo-Russian invasion of 1941. Reza's son, Mohammad Reza Pahlavi, became Shah upon his father's abdication and ruled Iran until the Islamic revolution in 1979.

[87] Ayatollah Mohsen Al-Hakim's son is Abdul Aziz al-Hakim. As of 2007, Hakim is the leader of the largest political party in Iraq, the Iraqi Council of Representatives. He formerly led the Iranian-based Iraqi expatriate party called the Supreme Council for the Islamic Revolution in Iraq.

[88] The Tabtaba'i family also claims direct family lineage to Hassan ibn Ali, viewed in the Shia tradition as the second Shia imam and early caliphate.

[89] This area is just west of the Iranian city of Mehran in the central sector.

⁹⁰ This area is about 50 miles northeast Ba'quba in the Diyala province.

⁹¹ Kurdish and Arabic names will differ a little. We understand this to be the Kurdish version; the Arabic seems to be Benjaween.

⁹² This "reserve force" was often a combination of local Ba'ath militia (including tribal militias in some areas), Quds militia, Fedayeen Saddam, and members of the local security office.

⁹³ Sayyid Qutb was an Egyptian Islamist and a leading intellectual for the Muslim Brotherhood movement until he was executed by Egypt in 1966. His writings have inspired a new generation of Sunni Salafi extremists, most notably al Qaeda.

⁹⁴ The history of Hamas is a topic of significant debate and rumor in the Middle East. It is generally accepted that Hamas was formed in late 1987 in Egypt by members of the Muslim Brethren. Its name is an acronym for *Harakat al-Muqawama al-Islamiyya* (Movement of the Islamic Resistance) which also means *zeal* in Arabic. Various sources report that Israel either founded or supported Hamas in its early days as a counterweight to the Palestine Liberation Organization's leadership.

⁹⁵ The General was referring to high ground just inside the Iranian border near Karand, Iran.

⁹⁶ For more information, see also Kevin Woods, *Iraqi Perspectives Project Phase II, Um Al-Ma'arik (The Mother of All Battles): Operational and Strategic Insights from and Iraqi Perspectives, Volume 1*, Institute for Defense Analyses Paper P–4217 (Alexandria, VA: Institute for Defense Analyses, 2007).

⁹⁷ General Hamdani may be referring to the original U.S.-provided Iranian C² system in existence under the Shah before the 1979 Islamic revolution.

Bibliography

Fontenot, Gregory, E.J. Degen, and David Tohn. *On Point: The United States Army in Operation Iraqi Freedom*. Annapolis, MD: Naval Institute Press, 2005.

Hamdani, Ra'ad. *Before History Left Us*. Beirut: Arab Scientific Publishers, 2006.
Hiro, Dilip. *The Longest War: The Iran-Iraq Military Conflict*. London: Routledge, 1991.

Nordeen, Lon O., Jr. *Air Warfare in the Missile Age*. Washington, DC: Smithsonian Institution, 1985.

O'Ballance, Edgar. *The Gulf War*. London: Brassey's Defense Publishers, 1988.

Pois, Robert and Philip Langer. *Command Failure in War: Psychology and Leadership*. Bloomington: Indiana University Press, 2004.

Powell, Colin L., "Remarks to the United Nations Security Council," New York City, February 5, 2003.

Soutor, Kevin. "To Stem the Red Tide: The German Report series and its Effects on American Defense Doctrine, 1948–1954." *Journal of Military History*, October 1993.

U.S. Department of Defense. Joint Publication 1–02, *Department of Defense Dictionary of Military and Associated Terms* (as amended through 12 July 2007). Available at <www.dtic.mil/doctrine/jel/doddict/>.

U.S. Government. "Iraqi Weapons of Mass Destruction Programs." February 13, 1998.
Woods, Kevin M. *Iraqi Perspectives Project Phase II, Um Al-Ma'arik (The Mother of All Battles): Operational and Strategic Insights from and Iraqi Perspectives*. Volume 1, Paper P–4217. Alexandria, VA: Institute for Defense Analyses, 2007.

Woods, Kevin M., et al. *The Iraqi Perspectives Report: Saddam's Senior Leadership on Operation Iraqi Freedom*. Annapolis, MD: Naval Institute Press, 2006.

Index to Themes in the Discussions

To facilitate finding a particular topic or theme, this index lists discussion topics alphabetically and indicates the page on which the topic is introduced.